MW00773609

HOUSING HUMANS

A Vicarious Memorandum

HOUSING HUMANS

A Vicarious Memorandum

Eugene E. Jones, Jr.

InTandem Digital Press

Housing Humans: A Vicarious Memorandum

Published by: InTandem Digital Press
https://www.intandemdigitalpress.com/

Cover design & all book illustrations by: Kima Lenaghan, kimalenaghan.com

Paperback ISBN: 978-1-7357781-0-5
Hardback ISBN: 978-1-7357781-1-2
eBook ISBN: 978-1-7357781-2-9
Library of Congress Control Number: 2020919775

Publisher's Cataloging-in-Publication Data

Names: Jones, Eugene E., Jr., author.
Title: Housing humans : a vicarious memorandum / Eugene E. Jones, Jr.
Description: Includes bibliographical references. | Atlanta, GA: InTandem Digital Press, 2020.
Identifiers: LCCN: 2020919775 | ISBN: 978-1-7357781-1-2 (Hardcover) | 978-1-7357781-0-5 (pbk.) | 978-1-7357781-2-9 (ebook)
Subjects: LCSH Jones, Eugene E., Jr. | Government executives--United States--Biography. | Housing policy--United States. | Home ownership--United States. | Leadership. | BISAC BIOGRAPHY & AUTOBIOGRAPHY / Personal Memoirs | POLITICAL SCIENCE / Public Policy / Social Services & Welfare
Classification: LCC JK723.E9 .J66 2020 | DDC 351.73092--dc23

Housing Humans

Self-actualizing people have a deep feeling of identification, sympathy, and affection for human beings in general. They feel kinship and connection as if all people were members of a single family. -Abraham Maslow

American psychologist and author, Abraham Harold Maslow created a *hierarchy of human needs* based on his theory of psychological health required for individuals to fulfill their innate human needs. His hierarchy of needs placed each in priority as essential for obtaining self-actualization.

In his hierarchy of needs, Abraham Maslow begins with human beings' most basic needs— our physical needs. Of those, shelter is the most basic. And without it, no human being can self-actualize. For 35 years, my commitment has been to treat residents as I would my mother, father, child, brother, sister—or anyone I care about and love. We often forget that those living in poverty are human beings with the same needs and wants as the rest of humanity.[1]

Dedication

My son, listen to your father's instruction,
and do not let go of your mother's teaching.
                                    Proverbs 1:8 NIV

To My Parents: The instructions and teaching my parents modeled throughout their lives set the foundation for who I am today as a son, parent, and community leader. My father's Air Force career provided so many learning opportunities that I still cherish today. My mother is a Proverbs 31 woman: honorable, active, wise, strong, and a wonderful wife and mother. I dedicate this book to them—Eugene E. Jones, Sr. and Kay Francis Jones—because their groundwork in raising me is what has guided and continues to guide me in my life.

*****

Whoever welcomes one of these little children in my name welcomes
me; and whoever welcomes me does not welcome me
but the one who sent me.
                                    Mark 9:37 NIV

To My Children, Oscar Geter, Rachel Kay Jones, and Eugene Jones III: You have made me stronger, better, and more fulfilled than I could have ever imagined. You are the beats in my heart, the pulse in my veins and the energy of my soul. Even as adults, remember that I will always be a call away when you need a listening ear. Don't ever hesitate to share with me the good or regretful things in your life. We are all humans; therefore, we make mistakes. God knows I have made my share of them. The important point of making mistakes is learning from them. My love for you is unconditional, and it will always be. Every single one of you is a glorious blessing in my life, and you will always be. I am proud and honored that I am your dad.

*****

Whatever you have learned or received or heard from me,
or seen in me—put it into practice.
Philippians 4:9a NIV

To My Mentor: Elizabeth "Betty" Lee Michael spent her career working as a civil servant at Kirtland Air Force Base, where I was stationed. Her family had immigrated to New Mexico in 1890 from Lebanon. She nurtured me, and I considered her a second mother. Betty taught me so many great things that have served me so well in life and work. A committed Christian, she modeled all the virtues described by Christ that one should have. Betty passed away Saturday, January 5, 2019, in Albuquerque, New Mexico.

*****

"Here's to strong women. May we know them.
May we be them. May we raise them."
Unknown

To all the women who crossed my life; My life has been enriched by women I worked with and worked for. I have never felt threatened by a woman who knew more than me. What I have done throughout my life is observe and learn from the women who have surrounded me. The learnings have been magnificent and valuable as a professional and father. My female teachers have been of all ages, ethnic background, diverse professions, and mothers. I want to thank them all because I am a better man for what they taught me.

*****

I firmly believe that our salvation depends on the poor.
Dorothy Day

Lastly, I dedicate this book to—human beings who have no home or lost their homes, have not been prioritized by our great nation, and face ongoing challenges. I see you. I know you. I continue to stand and speak for you and for all others who do not have a voice.

Eugene E. Jones, Jr.
Atlanta, Georgia,
August 10, 2020

Table of Contents

I: Finding My Way Here

II: My Call-to-Action:
Reforming National Housing Policy

III: Lessons in Leadership

Acknowledgments

There is nothing like a team that is determined, indomitable, and enthusiastic about what they are doing. An ambitious and driven team is a dream-team for any project or organization. My Gene's Dream Team was committed to excellence, assuring that all this book contains is truthful and reliable, empathetic to issues related to homelessness and housing, confident about the skills they brought to the project, communicative, uplifting each other, and a pleasure to work with throughout a year.

I wish to acknowledge those who helped make this book possible:

Silvia de la Fe Gonzalez, Albuquerque, New Mexico, founder and CEO of out-of-the-box initiatives, LLC, was responsible for leading Gene's Dream Team. She facilitated and coordinated the book project's team members' engagement, research, writing, editing, and organization. Silvia's background includes federal and local government service, publisher of a national magazine and a state-wide newsletter, executive producer and host of a TV Public Affairs show for WPLG-TV, an ABC affiliate, global non-profit consulting, and a deep commitment to serving the poor. As Chief Strategy Officer, Silvia's focus is to find ways to develop and grow the vision I have described in this book.

Patricia Wilson, Tennessee, was the first to join Gene's Dream Team as a researcher, transcriber, and copyeditor. Working as a virtual assistant for nearly 15 years, Patricia came with a host of impeccable gifts. She dug deep and created a collection of news clippings, interviews, videos, and other mediums beginning with my work in Kansas City to my most recent one in Atlanta. She was given the name of "Eagle Eye" because she identified the smallest grammatical or spelling error! Without Patricia's diligent, thorough, exceptional work, this book would not have been possible. Learn more about Patricia and her work via UpWork.

Dave Ficere, Arizona, founder of Ficere Writing Solutions, has over 30 years of experience as a writer and editor. Dave has worked with scores of individuals and companies, guiding them to improve their message and tell their story. His tagline is "Bringing Your Story to Life." He took my thoughts and helped synthesize and organize them by writing and editing much of what is in this book. You can find more information about Dave at www.daveficere.com.

Marc Brailov, Chicago, Illinois, Global Corporate Communications Consultant, has 20 years of successful experience and distinction in global corporate communications, public relations, media relations, marketing, and branding. He is highly entrepreneurial, creative, and proactive, with outstanding communications, management, strategic, and mentoring skills. Marc's strategic mind and tenacity made him an excellent and successful public relations consultant by obtaining interviews and getting my vision widely spread. He also served as a sounding board that brought clarity and insight into the book's vision. Learn more about Marc on LinkedIn.

Julia Maldonado is the Publisher of InTandem Digital Press and Founder of Atlanta's InTandem Digital Consulting. Julia was instrumental in all aspects of publishing for *Housing Humans*. She is a creative content writer, CX enthusiast, and social media guru. Julia is a passionate thought-leader dedicated to delivering best-in-class customer experiences. Julia did a phenomenal job on my website and in developing all social media platforms to ensure all of my thoughts and ideas were communicated appropriately. For more information about Julia's work or to contact her, visit: www.intandemdigitalconsulting.com.

Kima Lenaghan, Toronto, Canada, is an illustrator and ceramicist. She is fondest of worldbuilding, forming narratives and symbolism drawn from varied fields of research and experiences. Each illustration is preceded by journaling or a conversation. Her work is a eulogy to unanswerable questions, life on earth, and making meaning. She teaches Observational Drawing to illustration students at OCAD U, where she graduated from with a Design degree in Illustration in 2018. Kima did an extraordinary book cover design, drew the portrait of John Lewis in the book, and consulted with Julia on publishing steps. You can learn more about Kima's work by going to www.kimalenaghan.com.

Elvira Calizaire, Davie, Florida, is an ordained Minister, founder of Elvira Calizaire Ministries, who has a passion for intercessory prayer. In 2018, Elvira began a Prayer Line Ministry. Twice a week, more than 30 individuals connect on the phone to pray for the needs of individuals, our nation, and for special prayer requests. Her prayer support and encouragement enabled me to deal with some rough personal times and professional challenges. You can reach Elvira at Elviracalizaireministries@gmail.com

Your contributions to my personal life and this project are deeply appreciated. I look forward to our continued collaboration as we seek to develop and grow the vision this book presents. You have all been a blessing in my life.

Foreword

Former City of Chicago Mayor Rahm Emanuel (D):
Gene Jones first joined the Chicago Housing Authority in April 2015 as Chief Property Officer. Two months later, he became the Acting Chief Executive Officer, and in January 2016, I named him permanent CEO.

Gene's leadership's true measure is that he understood that CHA of old was just an isolated housing network of counted units. His passion for customer service made him think not only as a housing authority leader but also as a community builder. While he was in Chicago, Gene made sure housing units were located near libraries, grocery stores, restaurants, coffee shops, transportation centers, better schools, afterschool activities, and sports activities.

He made sure that public housing residents saw the same things in their neighborhood as they saw in every setting. They were no longer isolated geographically, psychologically, and physically. Gene did an incredible job of reinventing and reimagining public housing in Chicago.

He knew that if you're going to build a place where residents feel part of a neighborhood and a community, you have to have all the pillars that create a residential and retail economy.

For example, if you visit Woodlawn in Chicago today, you can find Mariano's and Jewel grocery stores, POAH (our new housing), a new school, a racquetball/squash facility, and mentoring. In the

Washington Park section of Chicago, we have the XS Tennis Facility, a new train station, Peach's Restaurant, and the University of Chicago. At the Ellis Park Facility in Bronzeville, CHA Financial Resources has located there just two blocks from Mariano's grocery store that it could finance by selling the land to Mariano's. In all three of these communities, population, jobs, and graduation rates are up. Crime is down in these three communities.

Gene's legacy has been to reinvent, rethink, and reimagine what a housing authority can be as he did at CHA. His book not only relates to his life, the lessons he learned in the military, and at the helm of nine housing authorities that included Toronto, Canada; it also has Gene's vision to reform the US housing policy. If you are working in any aspect of US housing, I recommend you read this book.

*****

Mayor Stephen Goldsmith, former Mayor of Indianapolis (R):
As Mayor of Indianapolis, I inherited a public housing authority that had been constantly troubled. It could not keep up with maintenance, had a number of problematic practices, constantly found itself troubled by HUD and so on. Too many lives were being adversely affected, and I pressed the Board for reforms and for the hiring of a competent professional—someone who understood housing, finance, HUD rules, and the needs of residents. We found Gene Jones.

We gave Gene total control over the reforms. I would shield him from political interventions (to this day I don't know his politics—don't care really), and he would professionally execute. There are folks who understand HUD. There are others who know how to lead and manage staff. And still others with sufficient empathy to understand residents and be impatient in the need to solve their problems. Gene was uniquely all three.

He shaped up the organization, reduced the
record time, produced one of the country's most :
VI projects that restored dignity for those living t\
surrounding neighborhood. To this day Gene remains
a respected professional and friend, but an example c
qualities in public service.

When you see something that is not right, not fair, not just, you have to speak up. You have to say something; you have to do something.

John R. Lewis

John Robert Lewis was an American statesman and civil rights leader who served in the United States House of Representatives for Georgia's 5th congressional district from 1987 until his death in 2020. He was the chairman of the Student Nonviolent Coordinating Committee from 1963 to 1966.

Preface

I've worked for 35 years leading housing authorities in nine U.S. cities and one in Canada. In all these cities, I was called to fix housing authorities experiencing a host of managerial and financial challenges. Throughout my career, affordable housing has never gotten the attention it deserves from either political party leaders. Now, I hope to help induce a call to action that can revamp our nation's housing policy.

We must speak up, but more importantly, we must act.

Two icons of social justice spoke up, but they coupled their beliefs with action. Dr. Martin Luther King, Jr. believed in work. He believed in engaged people. He preached the philosophy of nonviolence, but he also was a man of action.

The late Congressman John Lewis, like his mentor, Dr. King, believed in action, "We must never give up, or give in, or throw in the towel. We must continue to press on! And be prepared to do what we can to help educate, motivate, and inspire people to stay engaged and involved, and not lose their sense of hope. We must continue to say we're one people. We're one family. We all live in the same house. Not just an American house but the world house. As Dr. King repeatedly said, 'We must learn to live together as brothers and sisters. If not, we will perish as fools.'"

It is time to move urgently into action in creating not just housing but resident-focused neighborhoods. Dr. King's and Mr. Lewis' ideals have been my commitment to the residents I have served.

My vision is for a decisive-action, sustained-housing policy reform, organized by both the public and private sectors, and collectively led by like-minded individuals and groups committed to correcting the social injustice of severely unequal access to affordable housing.

Since you are reading this book, the topic of affordable housing must interest you. If so, consider becoming active in this social movement.

The affordable housing crisis did not become a significant issue of the 2020 political campaign despite multiple calls to action by reputable homelessness and housing state and national organizations. These campaigns, organized via social media and articles written by numerous, credible individuals or research entities, seemingly fell on deaf ears.

Yes, Democratic 2020 presidential candidates penned position papers on affordable housing. Despite this, the topic was not discussed in the debates nor on the campaign trail in a way that matched its high level of importance. It has neither ranked in the top 10 of the subjects discussed during the primary debates, nor has it been a high priority for the Trump Administration through early 2020.

As this book goes to print, housing is not a sufficiently high priority, nor is it an urgency. From our recent history, it appears that U.S. social ills must become devastating events to get adequate attention. We have COVID-19 and Black Lives Matter as two examples of local, state, and federal governments responding after disastrous events have occurred. The deaths of Eric Garner, Walter Scott, Jordan Edwards, Michael Brown, Akai Gurley, Tamir Rice, Freddie Gray, Philando Castile, Stephon Clark, Botham Jean, Atatiana Jefferson, Breonna Taylor, Ahmaud Arbery, and George Floyd all point to the problem found in inner-city neighborhoods throughout the U.S.

Intellectually, we know some people in this nation will have no place to live come October, November, and December of 2020. Still, we have lots of agencies advocating for quick fixes to deal with this issue. There is no long-term focus from governors, mayors, and Congressional members to gather housing authorities—practitioners—along with the most apparent Cabinet departments, to develop a nationally focused housing solution. Instead, it seems that the need for housing now will have to become a calamity of its own.

Affordable housing and homelessness are not just about building new dwellings or repairing old structures for housing needs. Along with construction and renovations, there needs to be the concurrent creation of neighborhoods and communities. These affordable housing communities need to be built to support residents and homeless people who have existed in abject poverty for too long.

Affordable housing is a much more complex crisis than how it is typically presented. Just ask inner city mayors who deal with gun violence, joblessness, health care, safety, and adequate transportation. They long to see schools of excellence and access to commodities like fresh food groceries, pharmacies, recreational parks, and the like.

After the housing crisis of 2008 and 2009, government leaders at the national level began looking more closely at the housing market. They asked themselves what could be done to tear down barriers that were preventing new housing start-ups. In September 2016, the Obama Administration released a "Housing Development Toolkit" designed to help state and local leaders surmount "local barriers to housing development." Toolkit's Executive Summary defined the problem this way:

> Over the past three decades, local barriers to housing development have intensified, particularly in the high-growth metropolitan areas increasingly fueling the national economy. The accumulation of such barriers – including zoning, other land use regulations, and lengthy development approval processes – has reduced the ability of many housing

markets to respond to growing demand. By modernizing their approaches to housing development regulation, states and localities can restrain unchecked housing cost growth, protect homeowners, and strengthen their economies.[1]

"A stable, functioning housing market is vital to our nation's economic strength and resilience," the report concluded. "Businesses rely on responsive housing markets to facilitate growth and employee recruitment. Construction workers, contractors, and realtors depend on stable housing markets to fuel their careers. And the availability of quality, affordable housing is foundational for every family; it determines which jobs they can access, which schools their children can attend, and how much time they can spend together at the end of a day's commutes."[2]

Writing this book was inspired by several factors in my life's trajectory, including my lifelong work helping communities fix their affordable housing crisis. I finished this book during the Coronavirus pandemic of 2020. More than 30 U.S. state governors and a multitude of mayors had issued a variety of stay-at-home orders. Some directed residents to stay at home altogether. Others recommended sheltering in place or staying at home except for essential tasks such as grocery shopping or visiting a doctor or working at jobs deemed critical.

It struck me that more than half a million American individuals and families in the U. S. did not have to ever worry about such orders. They had no home in which to shelter in place. It also meant that they would not have food or other basic needs that all of us need to bloom, thrive, and flourish.

The U.S. has a shortage of seven million homes—affordable and available rental homes—for extremely low-income households. Nationwide, there are approximately 1.3 million units of occupied public housing managed by some 3,400 public housing authorities (PHAs). Public housing differs in terms of the people who live there as well as the types, location, quality of the buildings, and the surrounding areas.

My housing career has been about fixing housing problems. However, it has also been about rethinking, revamping, and redoing housing as it has been known for decades. It has been about bringing commitment, compassion, understanding, positive energy, innovation, entrepreneurship, equality, and human-centered services to meet residents' needs.

Abraham Maslow demonstrated that without shelter, individuals could not self-actualize. They cannot thrive. They can neither grow personally nor professionally.

I am a living example of what can happen to an individual born into a low-income family if they are allowed access to all the necessary services and opportunities to become self-actualized. That means having access to education, employment, healthcare, and opportunities—all of which helped turn my life around.

Crucially, what led me to become a whole and successful person was an epiphany I experienced in Japan by exploring and becoming familiar with God. It is this relationship that has guided me and continues to oversee every aspect of my life.

Throughout my career, I've made it my mission to be hands-on in my work on behalf of people with housing needs. Wherever I've gone, I've always told my staff that "I'm not trying to operate this housing agency from behind a desk. They know I'm out there with the people we serve. And I'm not just going out there from 8 to 5. We're here to serve this community 24/7. I want you to base what you think of my word on my outcomes. I have a plan for results." A new one is urgently needed by our entire nation now.

— I —

Finding My Way Here

As kids, our experiences shape our opinions of ourselves and the world around us, and that's who we become as adults.

Chris Hemsworth

– Chapter 1 –

Motor City Madness

I was born on September 29, 1955, on Selfridge Air Force Base near Mount Clemens, Michigan—just outside of Detroit. I am the second of six children, with one older sister among the four girls and two boys in my family. Unlike many other families, the six of us were really close and did everything together. Even our birthday parties were family-centered because we were poor and couldn't afford to invite other people. I remember surviving on Carnation powdered milk, cabbage, cornbread, beans, spaghetti, and bologna. But life was good. We had a lot of fun and never realized we were poor. As siblings, we rarely argued or fought; and when we did, it was out of the earshot or sight of our parents, because once Mom got involved, that was the end of the argument!

Mom was the gatekeeper of the house, mostly staying at home, with some occasional outside work as a housekeeper, sometimes working weekends. With four of us kids one year apart and two separated by five years, our family had built-in babysitters. Mom ran a tight ship managing the house and us kids, and she didn't take crap from anyone. She made us work and learn life skills, such as ironing, cooking, and sewing. Even at a young age, I realized how valuable this training was, which became evident once I got older. Other young people didn't know any of these skills, but I could make a tight bed, put a crease in my trousers, and cook a decent meal.

While serving in the United States Air Force, my dad worked in accounting and finance. He was a disciplinarian, and the last thing you wanted to do was cross him or have any of your bad behavior get back to him. I never knew my grandparents on either side of the family and only met one grandmother a few times. I remember we called her "Bumma" because we couldn't say "grandmother." Other than that, they weren't part of our family growing up.

Despite being a good kid, I was a poor student who didn't apply himself and just wanted to have fun. I was a jokester who fudged my report card and just got by, getting Cs, Ds, and some Fs. I was pretty strait-laced and didn't drink or do drugs. We never went to church, but I think living and going to school on a military base helped keep me on the straight and narrow. I do remember one teacher, Ms. McGilicutty, who was short, blond, and a little overweight. She was kind and took an interest in me. I still remember her all these years later.

Growing up in a military family, everything was structured for us. We moved about every three years, depending on my dad's assignment. When I was five years old, we moved to Montana, where it seemed like we were the only black kids in the state! Although my entire school was white, it didn't make me feel inferior or different. We lived in a trailer on Malmstrom Air Force Base, located on the east side of Great Falls. The base is one of three U.S. Air Force facilities that maintains and operates the Minuteman III intercontinental ballistic missile. The 341st Missile Wing based there is charged with defending America with combat-ready airmen and nuclear forces.

In the Air Force, everyone was the same, and skin color didn't matter. Because we lived on the base, we were exposed to people and children of every nationality. I knew nothing about discrimination, even though it was the 1960s, a time when the nation was beginning to deal with racial discrimination.

In February of that year, four black students sat at a whites-only lunch counter at a Woolworth's in Greensboro, North Carolina, and were denied service. Their act of defiance triggered a wave of sit-ins for civil rights across the South. It brought national attention to the issue of racism that would continue throughout the decade. But

I did not experience any of that like I would have if we had lived off-base. We weren't exposed to other walks of life or low-income people. Now, we were considered low-income because my father was enlisted. However, we also got free housing and medical care, which helped improve our lifestyle.

I had a happy childhood, and I remember living next to a farm with horses in Montana. Dad would go outside to unfreeze the pipes during the cold winters. The snow would pile up underneath our trailer, freezing the pipes, and he had to go outside and shovel the snow away from the pipes so we could take a bath! Low temperatures ranged from the teens to 20s from November through March. The winters could be brutal at times, but I enjoyed our time there.

We left Montana and returned to Detroit in 1967, where I went to school on the base. During that time, I did join the Cub Scouts for about a year and earned some merit badges. However, I lost interest afterward and never went on to the Boy Scouts. I do remember especially enjoying Halloween. We would go everywhere with our pillowcases serving as candy baskets. People at all the stores, businesses, and homes gave out candy, and soon our pillowcases would be heavy and full of goodies!

I also went to Roosevelt Elementary School (since closed) in Detroit's inner-city, right next door to Central High School. Central was a notoriously bad high school, known as a place where students had to pay someone to leave them alone or give them protection. I had been sheltered from the real world while living and going to school on a military base, so going to a public school was an eye-opener for me. 1967 was the year of the famous riots in the Motor City. Also known as the "12th Street Riot," the July uprising was the bloodiest incident in what was later dubbed the "long, hot summer of 1967." The confrontations happened mostly between black residents and members of the Detroit Police Department. It exploded into one of the deadliest and most destructive riots in American history. When the dust had settled, 43 people were dead and 1,189 injured. More than 7,200 people were arrested, and more than 2,000 buildings were destroyed. Governor George Romney ordered the Michigan Army National Guard into Detroit. At the same time, President Lyndon Johnson sent in the United States Army's 82nd and 101st Airborne Divisions. I still remember seeing all of the planes landing at Selfridge and the troops who were sent in to deal with the rioters. I didn't understand the riots because it was so outside of my comfort zone.

I had a happy life, access to a swimming pool on base, and did not identify with the unrest in Detroit. Living on the base, we weren't exposed to the turmoil and rioting going on in the city, and I didn't understand why people were rioting. I enjoyed living in Detroit. The only regret I have about my time there (and elsewhere for that matter) is I can't remember who I grew up with because we moved around so much. If you grew up in a military family, you will understand. It was hard showing up mid-school-year, as the new kid; trying to make new friends; all while trying to figure out who the school bully was!

We weren't back in Detroit very long before dad was transferred to Yokota Air Force Base in Japan. The base is located on the Kanto Plain on Japan's largest island of Honshu, about 28 miles northwest of Tokyo. It was a beautiful location at the foothills of the Okutama Mountains. Yokota is both a United States and United Nations base and serves as the host base for Headquarters, United States Forces Japan, and the Fifth Air Force. Also, the 374th Airlift Wing, based at Yokota, provides tactical airlift, medical evacuation, and distinguished visitor airlift for the western Pacific region. This unit serves as a key strategic airlift hub for the entire area of operation.

I attended school in Tokyo and was exposed to a different culture as well as meeting a lot of embassy kids and experiencing old Japan. We had a cultural mix of students: Iranians, Chinese, Japanese, and people from all races and walks of life. From what I recall, we moved around in Japan, and I remember my dad trying to get on the waiting list for one particular housing area. Even though we lived on the base, we were surrounded by the entire Japanese community. It was fun to leave the base and sample the local food while getting immersed in

Japanese culture. I don't remember anything traumatic during our time in Japan, except an auto accident I had with some friends.

Four of us were crammed into a small car. I don't remember where we were headed. In Japan, the roads are so narrow that you have to pull off to the side to let cars headed the other way pass. We were going too fast (I was NOT driving) when the driver ran off the road and smashed into something. Everyone else in the car ran off, and I was left there alone. The Japanese police came and took a report, and I ended up going to the hospital. I didn't think it was a big deal, but my parents were upset at our recklessness. It was simply a case of young people fooling around—being stupid while driving. I stayed in the hospital overnight with stitches over my eye. I could have been partially blinded from it, but it was my only brush with the law. I was a good kid, who never smoked, took drugs, or got in legal trouble. I was always afraid of doing something to bring disrespect to my dad and family.

It was while we were in Japan that I began exploring my spirituality and started attending and getting involved in a Presbyterian church. I underwent a spiritual transition from having no knowledge about God to beginning to embrace faith as a practical part of my life. Even though I was living in Japan, which is primarily Buddhist, I never explored Buddhism but adopted a more Christian-centered faith. I continued going to church after we moved back to the United States and incorporated spirituality as part of my lifestyle. The church was also a gathering place on Sundays, which helped improve my social life.

One of the things I learned in Japan was how to respect people. Japan is quiet and moves at a much slower pace than America. To succeed there, you have to think strategically and plan. That became ingrained in me. I saw there was no discrimination, and people didn't care about color. As Americans living in a foreign country, we had to learn to represent ourselves and our country well, because people got their impressions about Americans from us and how we behaved. For example, when I lived in Germany in 1975, I saw many

7

Germans who hated Americans because of the disrespect they saw from American GIs. Many soldiers were lewd and took advantage of the local women, disrespecting them and sexually assaulting them. As a result, even if Germans spoke English, they would insist on you speaking German to them because of their disdain for Americans.

In 1971, we returned to the States from Japan, and I continued going to high school, attending Cody High on Detroit's west side. It was a nice neighborhood back then, located not far from Motown's historic district. But life was now totally different in Detroit. Here everything was black and white. It was unacceptable for blacks to associate with white people, and that was troubling to me as it was an entirely new experience and way out of my comfort zone. Since I had lived on-base among people of all races and cultures, I did not understand people not wanting to have any contact with other races. It was simply foreign to me.

In 11th grade, I had an epiphany of sorts. I decided not to be lazy anymore. I was instinctively a planner and knew I had the aptitude to succeed. I suddenly realized I needed good grades to get into college and began planning my life accordingly. From then on, I started applying myself scholastically and turned my performance around. I got As and Bs, with a focused goal of graduating so I could follow in my father's footsteps and join the Air Force. I graduated from high school in 1972, two years early, at the age of 16. While in high school, I played football and basketball. I didn't do well at football at 140 pounds with a thin build but excelled at basketball. I even played semi-pro ball as a point guard while I was in the military. But I never saw sports as an avenue to pursue beyond high school.

– Chapter 2 –

Into the Wild Blue Yonder

The Air Force was my only immediate goal, so in 1972 at the age of 17, I enlisted right out of high school. The Vietnam War was still going strong, and most young men my age did everything they could to avoid the military. The draft was still in force, and all 18-year-old men nervously watched each year as numbers were called. Those with high numbers were "safe," while those with numbers one to 20 knew they would be drafted. They often opted to enlist instead.

I was the polar opposite. I wanted to go to Vietnam because my dad had done two tours there. So, after enlisting, off I went to basic training at Lackland Air Force Base in San Antonio, Texas. Basic was easy, and I had a lot of fun because my dad had prepared me for it. I knew how to shine my shoes and what to expect.

> *Every Air Force journey is different, but no matter where your career takes you, every path begins in training. Each training program is designed to help you find your mental and physical strengths and to develop the skills and values necessary to succeed in the Air Force and achieve your goals. This is where you officially become an Airman.[1]*

After six weeks of basic training, I went straight to Sheppard Air Force Base in Wichita Falls, Texas, for 12 additional weeks of training. There wasn't much time to enjoy a social life, and I lost track of a lot of people I went to basic with, as we all scattered and went to different locations around the country. The Air Force had graded my aptitudes and recommended specific areas to pursue as a "best fit." I picked technical training for traffic and logistics management, which I felt would serve me well both inside the military and later in civilian life. From then on, all of my time and energy was focused on getting through technical school.

The Air Force not only teaches skill set development but leadership skills, such as how to think, plan, and execute strategies to accomplish the mission at hand. This model of leadership development is broken down into three levels: tactical, operational, and strategic. On the tactical level,

> *Air Force members master their primary duty skills. They also develop experiences in applying those skills and begin to acquire the knowledge and experience that will produce the competencies essential to effective leadership. Tactical leaders are the Air Force's technicians and specialists. At this level, airmen learn about themselves as leaders and how their leadership acumen can affect others. They are focused on honing followership abilities, influencing peers, and motivating subordinates.*

> *They are learning about themselves and their impact on others in roles as both follower and leader. They are being assimilated into the Air Force culture and are adopting the core values of their profession. They are gaining a general understanding of team leadership and an appreciation for institutional leadership. The tactical level includes gaining knowledge and experience in a primary skill, combined with educational and leadership training exercises.[2]*

At the operational and organizational level,

> *Air Force personnel should be able to understand the broader Air Force perspective and the integration*

of diverse people and their capabilities to execute operations. This level is where an Air Force member transitions from being a specialist to understanding Air Force integration. Based on a thorough understanding of themselves as leaders and followers, and how they influence others, they apply an understanding of organizational and team dynamics. They continue to develop personal leadership skills while developing familiarity in institutional leadership competencies. The operational level includes continued broadening of experience and increased responsibility within a related family of skills.[3]

And, finally at the strategic level,

Airmen combine highly developed occupational and enduring competencies to apply broad professional leadership capabilities. They develop and integrate deep understanding of Air Force missions and how tactics, techniques, procedures, technology, and people achieve synergistic results and desired effects, and also how the mission operates with interagency and multilateral relationships. At this level, an airman's required competencies transition from the integration of people with missions, to leading and directing exceptionally complex and multi-tiered operations. Based on a thorough understanding of themselves as leaders and followers, and how they apply organizational and team dynamics, they apply an in-depth understanding of leadership at the institutional and interagency levels. They achieve a highly developed, insightful understanding of personal and team leadership while mastering their institutional leadership competencies. The strategic level includes challenges to gain breadth of experience and leadership perspective (e.g., logical pairings of skills; educational opportunities and training focused on the institutional AF; joint, inter-government, business, and international views).[4]

After completing technical school in May of 1973, I picked two locations in California and one in Colorado as possibilities to continue my service. I did not get sent to any of these choices, ending up in Victorville, California. It is located in the western Mojave Desert of San Bernardino County and is considered to be High Desert and part of the so-called "Inland Empire."[5] It was not my first choice, but you go where the Air Force sends you. Despite my remote location, I was able to stay in touch with some of my friends. We had parted company after basic and had all gone to different technical schools around the country.

I was stationed at George Air Force Base, originally known as Victorville Army Airfield. The base was activated in 1941 to train pilots and bombardiers. After World War II, all flying operations were discontinued as part of a nationwide demobilization. The base was placed on standby status and used to store surplus B-29s, AT-7s, and AT-11s. Following the Korean War outbreak in 1950, the base was reopened and renamed George Air Force Base. Fighter pilots were trained in many different types of planes over four-plus decades at George.[6]

My group was in transportation, tasked with moving airplane parts and anything else that needed transporting around the world to support a wide range of missions. We also shipped household goods across the country for people serving in various branches of the military as well as some civilians. If it needed to go from point A to point B, we were responsible for all of it.

I didn't have a lot of time to socialize, and most of my high school buddies were in Los Angeles about two hours away by car. I would go visit them occasionally on the weekends, and we would hang out, but mostly I worked on the base. I needed something to fill my spare time, so I worked part-time as a waiter in one of the NCO clubs. After being stationed there for two years, I left Victorville in

1975 and moved to Frankfort, Germany. It was quite a culture shock moving from Southern California to Germany, but my older sister and brother-in-law were stationed at Rhein-Main Air Base, where I was, making my transition easier. Since this was my first time in Europe, it was nice to have someone to show me around and to help me get acquainted with a new area, in a different country and culture.

Rhein-Main was established in 1945. It served as the primary airlift and passenger hub for United States forces in Europe during its hey-day. Billed as the "Gateway to Europe" before closing in December 2005, the base became the primary American terminal in western Germany for the 1948 Berlin Airlift. The airlift was initiated after the Soviet Union blocked access to the three Western-held sectors of Berlin, deep within the Soviet-controlled zone of Germany. The Soviets cut off all rail and road routes through Soviet-controlled territory in Germany, prompting the famed airlift.[7]

I worked side-by-side with members of the military from other countries and different ethnic groups. The food was great, as was the nightlife in downtown Frankfort, and I also got to visit other cities, such as Amsterdam. But, as I mentioned before, many Germans still hated Americans, so you had to be on your best behavior and careful when venturing out.

I met this woman at the Drop-In Club in Frankfort, and we hung out together. I learned that she lived in an apartment complex of 400 women who all worked at the phone company. Needless to say, I hung out at the apartments a lot and dated several women. I did develop some relationships but nothing serious.

One day my supervisor came to me and said, "Hey Gene, we're going to close down this section that you're working in. Here are your options: You can go to Athens, Greece, or back to the States, but we're not sure where in the States."

"Hmm," I replied. "Let me think about that." It really wasn't much of a choice for me because it was another opportunity to explore a new part of the world. So, in 1976, I moved to Athens, Greece. During my time there, the civil war in Lebanon was raging. Many Americans were being evacuated from that war-torn nation. Tensions were heightened because the United States Ambassador, his economic advisor, and their Lebanese bodyguard-driver were killed during the violence in Beirut.[8]

In Washington, DC, politicians were especially sensitive to the plight of Americans living in Lebanon, and I was part of the team that helped with the transportation aspects of the evacuation. Many evacuees were sent to Crete or Italy, but not back to the United States. I had learned to speak Greek fluently, picking the language up quickly while living off base and dating Greek women. In fact, friends and co-workers used to jokingly call me "The Black Greek." I had a lot of fun in Greece, where I lived not far from the mansion belonging to Christina Onassis, the only daughter of the Greek Argentine shipping magnate Aristotle Onassis.

In 1977, I returned to the states and was stationed at Kirtland Air Force Base in Albuquerque, New Mexico. The base is best known for serving as the transportation center for Manhattan Project scientists in nearby Los Alamos during the development of the atomic bomb. After being overseas for two years, I was ready to return to the States and begin planning for life after the military. While stationed at Kirtland, I went back to school. I earned my Bachelor of Business Administration degree from the University of Albuquerque.

Kirtland was a huge base and had everything you could imagine. I continued working extra jobs on the weekends, bartending and serving as a maître d' at the Albuquerque Petroleum Club. Although you wouldn't think of Albuquerque as a place to meet celebrities, many famous people visited the club, which served the who's who of the business community. I met the owners and upper management people from the Smith's and Albertson's food chains, and they were always recruiting me to come work for them. The woman I worked for at Kirtland was the aunt to the Maloof family who owned the First National Bank and would later buy the NBA's Sacramento Kings. I was single, having fun, and not ready to get tied down yet, but it was nice to make such important connections.

I left Kirtland in 1981, returning to Sheppard AFB, where I worked until 1983. It was ironic returning there, since I had first been at Sheppard right out of basic training. I was coming full circle, and it seemed appropriate this is where I both started and ended my Air Force career. Everything at Sheppard was plain and simple. You worked to support the military all over the world, and they counted on you at all hours of the day and night for logistical support. I enjoyed making a difference and being part of such an important team. Still, I knew that after 10 years of service, it was time to end my military career.

I wasn't being challenged enough in the military, and the timing for Officer's Candidate School had not worked out for me. But I wasn't bitter I didn't get into OCS; I just saw it as a sign it was time to move on. I also realized I had been blessed in my military career with many choice assignments and locations. I knew the longer I stayed in, the more likely it was the law of averages would catch up with me. God had been good to me during my military career, and I wanted to go out on top, not in some assignment I hated. So, in 1983, at the age of 27, I was honorably discharged from the military and looked forward to my next adventure.

– Chapter 3 –

Groundbreaking Beginnings

After leaving the military, I received my Masters of Business Administration degree in 1984 from the Albuquerque extension campus of New Mexico Highlands University. Getting my MBA was the next step in getting out into the marketplace to test my skills.

While pursuing my MBA, I worked as a credit card supervisor at the First National Bank of Albuquerque. The woman I used to work with (who had a connection to the Maloof's) got me the job. Some people thought I was her inside man because the Maloof family owned the bank. I worked there for about 14 months while pursuing my MBA. From there, I went to Bellamah Community Development as an accountant. The land development company worked in Colorado, Arizona, Texas, and Oklahoma, and New Mexico. Fortunately, I did not have to do any traveling. My goal at that time was to get my license as a Certified Public Accountant. Working as an accountant for a major firm like Bellamah was a big step in that direction.

When I left Bellamah in 1985, I got a job as an auditor with the Office of Inspector General at the Department of Housing and Urban Development (HUD). That position, based in San Francisco, gave me workplace experience toward getting my CPA license. Off I went to the *City by the Bay*. The new job required quite a bit of traveling, and by 1989, I was at the point in my life where I was thinking about settling down. I was looking forward to getting married, buying a house, and starting a family.

I was in my 30s when I met a manager of one of the largest social security offices in the Bay Area. We began dating and were married in 1989. My new wife already had a three-year-old son, Oscar, from a previous relationship, so we had an instant family.

Another job opportunity came along that year as the controller for the San Francisco Housing Authority, and I took it. My wife and I bought a house across the bay in Oakland. It was a beautiful city, and I did not mind the commute across the Bay Bridge. The double-deck bridge was a part of Interstate 80 and the direct road between San Francisco and Oakland, carrying about 260,000 vehicles a day.

The year 1989 was significant for several reasons. There was marriage, a new job, relocating to Oakland, and the earthquake. On October 17, a 6.9 magnitude earthquake struck the Bay Area at 5:04 p.m., just minutes before the start of game three of the World Series between the San Francisco Giants and Oakland Athletics. The quake killed more than 67 people, injured another 3,000, and caused more than $5 billion in damages.[1]

My wife was seven-months pregnant with our daughter when the quake hit. I had left San Francisco for a meeting in Oakland and crossed the Bay Bridge about the same time that the ground began shaking. I no sooner got to the hotel for my appointment when an upper portion of the bridge collapsed, falling to the level below. I had just crossed the same bridge less than 30 minutes earlier.

Meanwhile, my wife had left work, but because there were no cell phones in 1989, I had no way of knowing whether she was safe, had been one of those killed, was trapped by collapsing bridges, or was stuck in traffic somewhere. I got ahold of Oscar, about 5:30, and learned he was okay at a relative's house about two miles from our home. We continued worrying about my wife.

There was so much road and bridge damage that she had to detour more than 50 miles south. She drove from San Francisco to San Mateo, crossed a different bridge to Haywood, and then turned north to Oakland. She walked through the door at 11:00 that night after driving more than six hours to get home. God was looking out for our family! Thankfully, the stress did not affect my wife's pregnancy, so our daughter, Rachel, was born on Christmas Day in 1989.

The trauma and aftermath of both the Route 880 and Bay Bridge collapses was impactful and snarled travel for nearly a month after the earthquake. Aftershocks went on for a few days, and we couldn't go to work. Everyone was skittish, just waiting for the shaking to begin again. Eventually, the Bay Area Rapid Transit (BART) trains began running, the ferries started up, and people found new routes to get across the bay via the San Mateo bridge. Life slowly returned to normal.

Another traumatic event happened in October of 1991 when a series of brushfires broke out and wreaked havoc across the region. The so-called "Tunnel Fire" or East Bay Hills fire roared through the East Bay region, killing 25 people and injuring 150 others. Among the 1,520 acres burned were more than 2,800 homes and another 437 apartment, and condominium units. The economic damage was estimated at $1.5 billion.[2]

I was coming across the freeway when the first brush fire broke out in Oakland. I drove right past it and saw the firefighters who were already on the scene. Eventually, the fire jumped Interstate 80 and spread north toward Berkeley. It crossed the 580 freeway devastating the Oakland Hills suburbs to the east. What was scary is that a portion of the fire came within a half-mile of our house.

While all of this was happening, I was thinking about running for Mayor in Oakland. I was doing a lot of community work and serving on some non-profit boards, so I was becoming well known. One of my fellow board members was the sister of Andrew Young, the former United States Ambassador to the United Nations and former mayor of Atlanta, Georgia. I had always wanted to get into politics. My strategy was to run for the school board and then—If I won—use that position as a launching pad for a mayoral run. I thought the city needed a change, and I was the person for the job, but it never came to pass. I moved out of state before I could even run for the school board.

One day I got a call from Jeffrey K. Lines, the president of TAG Associates near Boston. They specialized in low-income housing management and had previously worked with troubled housing authorities in Boston, Washington D.C., and San Francisco. U.S. District Judge Dean Whipple had placed the Kansas City Housing Authority into receivership and was about to put TAG in charge of running it. The Kansas City Housing Authority had the dubious distinction of being the first housing authority in history to be placed into receivership by the federal government.

Lines told me about his company's plans for Kansas City. He wanted me to come on board as the Executive Director of the Kansas City Housing Authority. Together we agreed and later publicly stated that we expected to make substantial progress within two years of taking over the troubled housing authority. Ultimately, our prediction came true.

So, in June 1994, I left the Bay Area for Kansas City, Missouri. TAG brought me in as their first full-time employee to run the beleaguered Kansas City Housing Authority.

In announcing my hiring, Lines told the press, "We would not have submitted a bid if we had not found a competent individual to run the authority."[3] That was me.

Unfortunately, my wife did not want to leave her prestigious job in the Bay Area. We soon parted ways, divorcing in 1996. But I kept in touch with my two kids, bringing them out to visit, or I would hop on a plane myself to see them. They liked the visits to Kansas City and saw the trips as new adventures to enjoy.

The housing authority in Kansas City was a troubled agency, financially and operationally. People in the city did not trust them, so Judge Dean Whipple stepped in. The city needed to build mixed-income and affordable housing, but things were such a mess that it just wasn't happening. The agency had not gone bankrupt but received poor marks. For example, on HUD's grading scale, an agency with a 60 and above score was deemed a standard performer. An agency with a score of 80 and above was a high performer. When I arrived, Kansas City's score was 38. They ranked in the bottom third of all housing authorities in the country.

Because I had seen the HUD information about Kansas City, I knew what I was walking into. We had to improve the score and get the housing authority to at least the standard performer's level and a score of 60. Among the other issues were terrible morale among the staff, inconsistent leadership, and generally poor performance. Before taking the job, I had to be interviewed by a group of people, and everyone liked my approach. I was personable, expressed care about the staff, and wanted to build a team environment. They were welcoming to me and the methodology I use in dealing with staff. I went in with the idea of utilizing the skills, talent, and experience people there already had. I also wanted them to know I would be there for them. Managing people was the key. Most people want to be challenged and appreciated. With that, I was able to win over the staff and build team comradery.

I won over others as well, such as Mayor Emanuel Cleaver. He had no control over the housing authority once it went into receivership. Still, I kept him in the loop, and we had a good working relationship. He eventually left Kansas City, and as of this writing serves as a Congressman representing Missouri's 5th District. I attempted to keep everyone informed, including the state's congressional delegations and others in authority. I became friends with Congresswoman Claire McCaskill and others in government, including Missouri's governor, Mel Carnahan.

It took us about two years to get to the standard performer level, and HUD was thrilled to see the progress we had made. Although we educated the judge about the points system, he kept the housing

21

authority in receivership. As I later learned that decision was made because it benefitted the Legal Aid Society of Western Missouri. They were the ones who represented the plaintiffs in the petition before the federal court to put the housing authority into receivership. In my opinion, they kept the Kansas City Housing Authority in receivership for far too long. Incidentally, they were still in receivership for ten years *after* I left!

– Chapter 4 –

My Career—My Passion

I was happy in Kansas City and not looking to move when I got a call from the director of human resources for the city of Indianapolis, Indiana. She said the mayor wanted to talk to me about taking over their housing development department. So, I flew to Indianapolis and met with the mayor and his people.

"What would it take for you to come to Indianapolis?" they asked me. I gave them some outrageous criteria, knowing they would never go for it. We shook hands, and I returned to Kansas City.

I was shocked when Indianapolis officials called back a short time later and agreed to all of my terms. They had called my bluff, but because I'm a man of honor when I make a promise, I follow through on it. I had no choice but to accept the job.

In June 1997, I packed up and left for the city dubbed the Crossroads of America to run the largest housing authority in Indiana. In fact, throughout my entire career, every housing authority I've ever run has been the largest in its particular state. One bright note was that I had a good friend from Japan living in Indianapolis, so I knew somebody there.

HUD had scored the housing authority in Indianapolis as borderline. By the time I got there, it was in trouble. I had seen this in Kansas City and other places and knew what I had to do. When I arrived, the Indianapolis Housing Authority only had an interim director, so I jumped right in and got to work.

The Kansas City Housing Authority was under federal receivership when I got there. By contrast, Indianapolis was controlled by the local political structure, including the board of commissioners and the mayor. My team and I developed a good partnership with Republican Mayor Steve Goldsmith and the governing authorities, most of whom were also Republicans. Normally, public housing is steeped in politics, but Mayor Goldsmith didn't care about that. He just wanted to fix the problems. The only "politics" involved the mayor and others in the GOP trying to recruit me to join their political party. I wasn't interested in that.

The city had some great housing units as well as a large minority population of mostly African Americans. Our agency also transformed many neighborhoods with the mayor's help and blessing. He was very accessible, and together, Mayor Goldsmith and I wrote the "Home Rule" legislation in 1998 that is still on the books in Congress. The regulations gave block grant money to each state, allowing them to divide the funds locally to serve their communities.

"Every city across the country has public housing and money available. What we wanted to do was leverage the public dollars to generate more private money. That, in turn, could be used to fund housing needs in our community," Mayor Goldsmith said.

Although many cities have Community Development Block Grants available, the Home Rule legislation never went anywhere, because it got bogged down in politics. Despite that setback, we were able to close one of the city's troubled HOPE VI housing sites and get the Indianapolis Housing Authority off HUD's troubled list in two years.

Apart from work, my youngest son, Eugene, was born in Indianapolis in 1998, although his mother and I were never married. He lived with his mom during my time in Circle City as the natives called it.

In 2000, Mayor Goldsmith decided not to run for re-election, and the incoming mayor chose not to renew my contract. So, I knew it was time to move on and leave on top with no scandals. That was the way I liked to do things. So, I left Indianapolis and began my own consulting business. Among my clients was a HUD division that worked with troubled housing agencies. I worked as a consultant for cities in New Mexico, Alabama, California, Connecticut, and many more between 2000 and 2007. One of the many places I was employed during this time was Louisiana—where the (as of 2016) costliest hurricane to make landfall in the United States wrought catastrophic devastation.

– Chapter 5 –

The Perfect Storm

It was August 23, 2005, roughly eight months into my new job working in the Big Easy for the Federal Government's Department of Housing and Urban Development—HUD for short. As a deputy administrative receiver, I worked at the Housing Authority of New Orleans. HANO, as it is known, was in receivership and under the control of HUD. The federal agency was helping them build housing sites under the government's Homeownership and Opportunity for People Everywhere grant program, known by the acronym HOPE VI.

Katrina formed on Tuesday, August 23, 2005 as tropical depression #12 in the Atlantic. The next morning, the depression had strengthened into a tropical storm and was given the name "Katrina". Shortly after becoming a category 1 hurricane on Thursday, August 25, Katrina made landfall over South Florida around 6:30 pm EST between Aventura and Hallandale, Beach. At landfall, she had winds of 80 mph and a very well-defined eye.

Conditions were primed not only for strengthening, but rapid intensification. When Katrina moved into the Gulf of Mexico, the atmosphere was characterized by large-scale weak shear, very warm sea surface temperatures, and the aforementioned Gulf Loop Current. Her first period of rapid intensification was on Saturday, August 27 when she was upgraded to a category 3 (major hurricane) status. After stabilizing for 18 to 20 hours, she entered a second period of rapid intensification which began around 7 pm CDT on Saturday August 27.

Just 6 hours later (approximately 12:40 am Sunday, August 28, 2005), she had strengthened to category 4 status (maximum sustained winds of 145 mph). In yet another 7 hours, she had intensified to category 5 status (7 am CDT 8/25/05), and by 1 pm CDT she had maximum sustained winds of 175 mph (gusts to 213 mph). Her central pressure was 902 mb, the 4th lowest ever recorded in the Atlantic basin up to that point (a record that would be surpassed just a few weeks later by Hurricanes Rita and Wilma).

On the morning of Sunday, August 28, 2005, nearly 24 hours before landfall, Forecaster Robert Ricks at the National Weather Service in Slidell issued a very rare, dire warning to the residents of Louisiana.[1]

That "dire warning" led Mayor Ray Nagin to order the first-ever mandatory evacuation of New Orleans. He called Katrina "the storm that most of us had long feared."[2]

Part of that evacuation responsibility landed on my shoulders. I took all the payroll records and staff contacts and coordinated the efforts for our staff to leave for evacuation centers in Houston, Dallas, Galveston, and Atlanta. FEMA helped find housing for them, and I'm proud to say that all of our employees got paid even amidst the chaos that Katrina was causing. This relocation was a vital first step in allowing us to continue functioning to serve the needs of those in New Orleans who were about to be made homeless by Hurricane Katrina.

Mayor Nagin's evacuation order came a full 24 hours before Katrina's expected landfall. The possibility of a devastating hurricane was deemed a *potential catastrophe* because 80 percent of the New Orleans metropolitan area is below sea level. Emergency management officials in the city feared that the storm surge could crest over the protective levees, causing major flooding.[3]

Studies from both the Federal Emergency Management Agency (FEMA) and the Army Corps of Engineers had come to the same conclusion. A direct hurricane strike on New Orleans could lead to massive flooding. Such flooding, they cautioned, would lead to thousands of deaths from drowning and the suffering of thousands more from disease, homelessness, and dehydration as floodwaters receded and residents faced the storm's aftermath.[4]

As predicted, Hurricane Katrina devastated New Orleans. The Big Easy was spared a direct hit from the intense winds but succumbed to a different threat. As feared, the levee systems that held back the waters of Lakes Pontchartrain and Borgne were completely overwhelmed by an estimated 10 inches of rain and Katrina's storm surge. Eventually, as the levees gave way, 80 percent of the city ended up underwater.[5]

No one knew how to prepare for such a storm or what to do about the levees. New Orleans city officials were not even talking about them. As a result, no one took the blame when the levees collapsed, and everyone pointed fingers at someone else.

Although more than one million people left New Orleans ahead of the storm, tens of thousands could not or would not leave. Instead, they remained in their homes or sought shelter at the New Orleans Convention Center or the Louisiana Superdome. Thousands were left homeless by Katrina, which caused an estimated $160 billion in damages.[6]

As it often does after a major catastrophe, the federal government stepped in to help the residents of New Orleans and other cities devastated by Katrina. HUD was in the middle of that effort. The agency, under the leadership of Secretary Alphonso Jackson, launched two emergency voucher programs. HUD also offered unprecedented mortgage assistance and helped state and local leaders begin long-term disaster recovery.[7]

"HUD is in this for the long haul," Jackson told a Senate committee. "Providing short-term and permanent housing solutions for these families and assisting the states in the region with the challenges of long-term recovery are my highest priorities."[8] He added that the agency was "working overtime" to help find housing for HUD clients and to assist in the long-term recovery in the region.

There was one humorous exchange that came out of the relocation chaos. As I was working to help get some of my people from New Orleans to Galveston, the first thing they asked me was, "Gene, what if another hurricane comes?"

"Do you know what?" I responded. "There's not going to be another hurricane. Hurricane Katrina was the largest."

What did I know? I no sooner uttered those words when Hurricane Rita hit the Texas Gulf Coast less than one month after Katrina, devastating Galveston. I'm sure some of those who we moved there were cursing my name. Right then and there, I decided to give up weather forecasting!

Once Rita hit, we were forced to close our Galveston center and migrate to Dallas. Unfortunately, what was usually a four-hour trip took 24 hours because a lot of other people had the same idea. The roads were clogged, and gasoline was in short supply. Restaurants were closed. There were people stranded on the side of the road or camped out in the median because they ran out of gas.

But let's back up a bit. I first arrived in New Orleans in December 2004, eight months before Katrina hit the city. Before Katrina, I was responsible for the financing and development of low-income housing. That included the rehabilitation and mixed-income development of these sites, which sadly, were later devastated by Katrina.

New Orleans' public housing history is complex, amidst both economic and social challenges, HANO was tasked with providing much-needed housing as well as giving the poverty-stricken citizens a sense of community. [9]

After passing the U.S. Housing Act of 1937, the federal government began funding both the construction and operations of low-income housing. The first public housing developments began springing up in the 1940s. They consisted mostly of low-rise red brick type structures in "superblock" configurations. By the 1970s, these public housing units in New Orleans had deteriorated to the point that they were no longer livable under any reasonable standards. [10]

The HOPE VI grant program was introduced by HUD in the early 1990s to fund the redevelopment of distressed public housing sites. The idea was to reconfigure these sites into more traditionally designed neighborhoods to meet the needs of various income groups. The HANO website explains it this way:

> *This model encouraged higher quality construction, and the design of street patterns that would integrate the site into the fabric of the surrounding neighborhood. HANO and other housing authorities across the country contracted private developers and property managers to enhance the long-term viability of these new communities. Since the late 1990s, HANO has redeveloped several of its public housing sites under this model.* [11]

HUD's HOPE VI was a new approach to the challenge of public housing. One writer defined it this way:

The idea was to "deconcentrate" the poverty that beset older projects by employing the basic tenets of the emergent New Urbanist movement: a walkable grid of single-and multi-family homes that encourage street life. Huge and hulking projects would be torn down and replaced by smaller units that matched the scale of the neighborhood.[12]

This type of redevelopment was happening in New Orleans before Katrina. It continued after the hurricane destroyed much of what had already been built.

We began working with New Orleans city officials and the local police department when we knew Katrina was on its way. But no one knew or was prepared for what was to come.

I was in Sacramento on business when Katrina made landfall off the Louisiana coast on August 29, 2005, as a Category 3 storm with winds as high as 120 miles per hour. I couldn't get a flight directly to New Orleans because all flights had been canceled. Instead, I returned to the Houston command center where, as eyes and ears on the ground, I helped coordinate the HUD programs.

Three days later, I drove back to New Orleans and lived in Kenner, just three blocks from Lake Pontchartrain and the airport. I remember seeing blue tarps everywhere and the endless piles of debris—some of it two stories high. In addition, everyone was carrying a bag of belongings and looking for shelter. I'll never forget those canvas bags. There was a lot of looting, and some stuff was stolen from my townhome. Even though I lived close to the lake, there was not one drop of water in my unit. I was truly blessed!

We received a lot of help from officials in the cities where our evacuation centers were located. However, some of them helped us only because they saw federal money coming their way. FEMA and other federal government agencies would be allocating millions of dollars in post-Katrina aid, and some cities lined up for the gravy train. Houston city officials took control of the evacuation and relocation situation because New Orleans' city officials were nowhere to be found, having fled the city. Houston authorities stepped into the void, housing evacuees in the Astrodome and providing what the storm refugees needed.

Back in New Orleans, I talked with people from FEMA, and we came up with a strategy to relocate people who had fled to Houston. I helped administer those efforts in conjunction with local authorities as the middleman. The work involved a lot of phone calls, face-to-face communication, and driving around. Communication was vital, but difficult, because comm systems were down in many areas. Because I had an out-of-town area code, my phone worked when a lot of people with local area codes had no phone service. We used what phone lines were available, walkie-talkies, fax machines, and a lot of face-to-face communication. My staff and I collaborated with major city agencies to locate affordable housing for up to 60,000 displaced residents.

Operating amidst such chaos, we were constantly asking ourselves, "What do we do? What's next?" My role upon returning to New Orleans was the same—trying to find housing for the residents. I also wanted our staff back in New Orleans to work with FEMA. Most of them moved back, but there was no housing for them unless they lived far away from the flooding.

Coordination between federal departments, such as defense and transportation, was lacking in Katrina's aftermath. Those local officials who were still in New Orleans were overwhelmed.

Further complicating the problem was the fact that all the pre-storm weather forecasts were wrong, and New Orleans residents had been given a false sense of security.

Many people could not leave, and others chose not to. Those residents had to hunker down and try to survive. Many who did not leave died when the levees broke and the city flooded. I'll never forget the scenes after Katrina hit and the levees collapsed, flooding the city: the stench from sewage; the lack of showers and basic necessities like diapers; all the animals and critters roaming around the city; the smell and debris everywhere; and thousands of people homeless and living in the Super Dome.

FEMA was not prepared for Katrina. Everyone remembers the famous trailers with formaldehyde and the busses that were not utilized and left standing in the floodwaters. By their own admission, they were overwhelmed, and their plan was not adequate to respond to a hurricane of that magnitude. It was the first time they had dealt with a major catastrophe and had to play the politics of trying to appease the local authorities and other officials. FEMA's own internal report admitted it was almost three days before they realized the scope of the hurricane's destruction.

"The federal government, in particular the Federal Emergency Management Agency (FEMA), received widespread criticism for a slow and ineffective response to Hurricane Katrina. Much of the criticism is warranted," Department of Homeland Security Inspector General Richard L. Skinner wrote in a 218-page report reviewing the agency's handling of Katrina.[13]

Because most of New Orleans is below sea level, many of HANO's housing projects were destroyed by Katrina's devastating storm surge. HANO implemented a massive redevelopment program to both replace and modernize the 1940-era housing that Katrina destroyed. HUD authorized funding to totally raze and rebuild four primary public housing sites as well as continue to build and redevelop several more.[14]

If you've been to New Orleans since Katrina, you've seen that what they built after the hurricane are really sticks. They're not what most people would call quality housing. Now, if you want to go toe to toe with me over this statement, you can. But I worked down in New Orleans, and I've seen what we've done and what we've lost in that city. I think what they built back after Katrina is something they're going to have to rebuild in the next 15 to 20 years, if not sooner.

– Chapter 6 –

Back Home for Awhile

By 2007, I was tired of scrambling for business and the travel involved with being a consultant. With three kids, I needed a stable job with benefits. So, I began looking around for a city that could use my help on a more long-term basis. The answer came from my hometown— Detroit.

The Motor City's Housing Commission had a troubled history dating back to the 1990s. HUD nearly took over the Detroit Housing Department in 1995 during Mayor Dennis Archer's term. However, that scenario was partially averted because of Archer's close relationship with then-HUD Secretary Henry Cisneros. The next year, the Housing Department was rebranded as the Detroit Housing Commission (DHC). Less than one year later, HUD removed the commission from its troubled list for the first time since 1979. HUD later threatened to withhold $46 million for Detroit programs because the city had so badly mismanaged previous grant money— funds that had been originally awarded for tasks such as demolishing vacant buildings and removing lead paint from houses.[1]

The federal government did take control of Detroit's public housing agency in July 2005. That move came after decades of frustration over what it called the agency's money mismanagement and poor leadership that left thousands of Detroit residents living in crumbling, rat-infested buildings. Residents often complained about broken elevators, leaking or broken plumbing, rodents, and other deplorable conditions. The complaints continued even after federal money was poured into renovating the buildings.[2]

I was working as a consultant for another company, and one of their clients was the Detroit Housing Commission. Because I had seen their numbers, I knew where they were lacking and what I would be getting into if I took over. In October of 2007, I began serving as the executive director of the Detroit Housing Commission.

Much of what was wrong in Detroit centered around Mayor Kwame Kilpatrick. He and a development partner-friend cooked up what was discovered to be a crooked deal regarding Hope VI housing sites. I came in, documented everything about the dubious agreement, and straightened out the mess. I was even called before the grand jury to testify. The result led to Mayor Kilpatrick's downfall.

Kwame Kilpatrick resigned as mayor in September 2008 after being convicted of perjury and obstruction of justice. He was sentenced to four months in jail, but was released on probation after serving 99 days. In 2013, he was convicted on 24 federal felony counts, including mail fraud, wire fraud, and racketeering. That same year, he was sentenced to 28 years in federal prison.[3]

Businessman Dave Bing was the next mayor, filling in as interim mayor after Kilpatrick resigned. Bing was a home-town hero, having played for nine seasons for the NBA's Detroit Pistons before retiring and going into business. After he became mayor, Bing embarked on a learning curve, because he knew nothing about our agency and what we did. He trusted that I knew what I was doing and did not try to boot me out, even though I wasn't part of his staff. He knew we had done great things for the Detroit Housing Commission despite the city's housing agency being put under HUD receivership. We managed to fix enough of Detroit's housing problems within two to three years to get the DHC off the troubled list.

We did a lot of great things in Detroit and with the city's Social Services agencies. Among our accomplishments was the building of a development called Emerald Springs on the East Side of Detroit. The area, located in the worst part of town, was plagued by blight. Demolished housing developments lay dormant. No one thought we could turn that area around, but working together, we did it. The DHC also developed a great partnership with Detroit Edison and worked with them to redevelop the utilities and reinvest in those communities. By 2012, things had improved significantly in Detroit's public housing sector, and I sensed that it was time for a new challenge. Little did I know it would take me north of the border.

– Chapter 7 –

Turmoil in Toronto

A national search firm in Canada contacted me when I was working in Detroit about possibly heading north of the border. The city of Toronto needed someone who thought differently and wanted to get moving on a big housing project they had. I sent them some information, and we began talking in March of 2012. By April, they had picked me from among several candidates. It wasn't long before I was headed 230 miles northeast to one of Canada's premier cities.

I began working as the chief executive officer for the Toronto Community Housing Corporation (TCHC) in June of 2012.

I was the first American to run the largest housing authority in Canada and the first American to ever run a housing authority outside of the United States. I was also the first African American to do any of that as well. I took on these challenges because I wanted to see if the skills I had learned in the U.S. could transfer to a foreign country.

My hiring "raised some eyebrows," according to the *Toronto Star*.[1] They asked about negative feelings some people in Toronto had about the TCHC bringing in an American to fix housing issues in the city.

"There are always going to be naysayers, so you have to prove them wrong. That's the challenge," I told the *Star*. "I think I'm the right fit for Toronto Community Housing Corp. You're going to see tangible results real quickly."[2]

I was recruited to Toronto by Mayor Rob Ford to be responsible for all aspects of the TCHC operations. That included administration, management, development, financial control, and the development of all policies affecting the housing authority. Our agency was also tasked with delivering resident services, including case management, housing locator help, and employment resources for homeless veterans and others. The goal of these programs was to help improve and create self-sufficiency and enhance stable housing.

The agency had suffered from poor leadership and instability. I was the first person to permanently fill the top spot since early 2011 after audits exposed lavish staff spending and questionable procurement practices by my predecessor. The TCHC received 120 applications for the position and interviewed seven candidates before choosing me.[3] Bud Purves, the chairman of the TCHC board of directors, said hiring me was part of what he termed "transforming Toronto Community Housing into a respected housing agency."[4]

The TCHC is the second largest public housing provider in North America, with over 58,000 units. They own more than 2,200 buildings, including high-, mid-, and low-rise apartments, townhomes, and houses. At the time I took over, TCHC had 1,500 employees and an operating budget of $900 million.

Our agency managed eight major simultaneous housing projects, including several multimillion-dollar developments totaling 45,000 units. We also developed plans and negotiated an additional budget of over $150 million from the provincial government and the city of Toronto. We utilized the increased revenue to refinance existing mortgages by building strong and long-standing relationships with numerous agencies and key stakeholders. Working with those in the financial community, we improved TCHC's bond rating from BB to AAA. We did this by strengthening the agency's long-term economic stature while increasing our capital budget by 200-percent to bring the agency's housing inventory into compliance with current housing codes.

"I don't operate this agency from behind the desk," I told one group shortly after taking the position. "I have good staff, and I have great residents. Now, do we need better leadership? Yes. And that's why I'm here."

"My predecessors were about bricks and mortar," I told one reporter. "You weren't supposed to go into buildings. But my view is you've got to walk the stairways and knock on the doors."[5]

"People call me arrogant. They call me egotistical. They call me all kinds of names," I told a gathering at a neighborhood recreation center in a community high-rise. "But they know I'm a man of my word, I don't make promises I don't keep, and if I make a promise, I stand behind my promise. You'll always get that from me. I'm always honest. I don't procrastinate. When I say I'm going to do something, I'm going to do it."[6]

My time in Toronto was not without controversy. Things began unraveling in 2014, over management and staff changes I began making after arriving. In February 2014, I was denied my annual bonus, assigned a management coach, and forced to sign up for an executive leadership program. The TCHC board took the unusual action after their internal investigation said I "violated the public landlord's policies and 'failed to exercise proper management oversight.'"[7]

According to press accounts regarding the sanctions, "numerous TCHC employees complained to city officials about Jones's personnel methods since he began a broad management shakeup upon his arrival in mid-2012". The investigation that led to the sanctions focused on two recent allegations from internal whistleblowers.[8]

I left Toronto in April 2014 over what the press termed questionable hiring practices. The *Toronto Globe and Mail* wrote: "Mr. Jones's leadership has been under scrutiny over his hiring and firing practices—especially after a report from the city's ombudsman this week accusing him and other TCHC leaders of running the organization 'like their own personal fiefdom.'"[9]

City of Toronto ombudsman Fiona Crean pointed to a 67-percent turnover rate amongst staff since my arrival, resulting—according to the ombudsman report—in $1.6 million in severance costs. Crean accused other senior managers and me of an "abject failure of leadership for ignoring rules to promote, hire and fire staff seemingly at their own whim."[10]

TCHC board chair Bud Purves announced that vice-president Greg Spearn had replaced me as interim CEO as part of a "mutual agreement" and a $200,000 settlement.[11] "After much deliberation, the board and Gene have mutually decided that a change in leadership will best position Toronto Community Housing to move forward in implementing its strategic plan," Purves said in announcing my departure.[12]

My only public response to the controversy came in a statement through my lawyer, released to the press. It simply said, "Mr. Jones is pleased to state that the parties came to mutually agreeable financial terms last night."[13]

"This is one of the worst days in Toronto's history, losing a man of this caliber," Mayor Ford told reporters during a personal visit to TCHC headquarters. "It's unbelievable how people can be treated when they're trying to do better for the poor in this city."[14]

All I can tell you about my departure is that I can defend everything I've done in every city I've been in. No one on any of my staffs can say I cheated anyone, stole from anyone, or did anything inappropriate. Nothing on my record hindered or prevented me from taking the next opportunity or job. I'm very credible, and I rest on those morals. And when I say something's going to be done, it's going to get done-every time.

– Chapter 8 –

Chi-Town

I always tell people to be careful what you ask for, because I am one person that is going to tell you how I feel. I'm not going to sugarcoat it or anything like that.

After the turmoil in Toronto, I went back to my hometown of Detroit for a while, to figure out my next move. One day, Lawrence Grisham, a friend, whom I knew from the Detroit Housing Commission, called. He told me about a job in a new city.

"Gene, Chicago needs your help," he said.

"Okay, what would they like?" I asked.

"They need you in development and construction."

"Well, I'm not going as an employee and only as a consultant if I go anywhere."

"Okay. You're not going to be number one," Grisham responded.

"I'm not trying to be number one anywhere. I'm 61 years old. I'm tired. I'm not tired of social housing, but I don't want to be number one. I want to be in the background because if you know my history, that last one was a doozy," I told Grisham, adding, "Okay, I'll come."

So, I went to Chicago in April of 2015 to work in the area of public housing real estate. I was needed in that capacity because my boss had no experience building housing, and I did.

I got to know Megan Hart, who was the liaison between the city and the Chicago Housing Authority. Without my knowledge, she went to Mayor Rahm Emanuel one day and said, "You need to hire this guy." Soon after that, a member of the mayor's staff approached me. "Mr. Jones, the mayor wants you here on Friday with your resume and vetting slip."

"Okay," I said, not knowing what was happening.

I showed up for my appointment, and Mayor Emanuel got right to the point. "I want to make some changes. I want you to be the acting CEO [of the housing authority]." That was in June of 2015.

"Gene Jones has a proven track record of being a solution-driven leader in public housing," the mayor said in announcing my appointment. "Throughout his 30-year career, Gene has dedicated himself to providing residents' quality, safe, and affordable housing opportunities while building strategic partnerships with community organizations and promoting private sector investment in public housing. His expertise leading public housing authorities across the county is unprecedented, and he will be an incredible asset to Chicago."[1]

I was so grateful to Mayor Emanuel. I was thankful he had enough confidence and belief in me and my ideas to lead the Chicago Housing Authority. Under his leadership, I felt that the city could create new housing opportunities in every neighborhood.

Rahm Emanuel came to Chicago in 2011 as the Windy City's 55th mayor. He had served as a member of the United States House of Representatives between 2003 and 2009, and as White House Chief of Staff for President Barack Obama from 2009 to 2010.

The Chicago Housing Authority (CHA) is the second-largest public housing agency in North America and serves more than 20,000 low-income households. As the largest landlord in Illinois, CHA manages more than 100 properties consisting of over 25,000 homes and apartments. With a staff of 2,000 employees and contractors and a budget of more than $1 billion, CHA delivers mixed-income-focused affordable housing to help families and build vibrant communities.

Mayor Emanuel once said his goal was "to ensure that every resident in every neighborhood of Chicago has an opportunity to participate in the future that we are building in Chicago, and by working together, we can make that goal a reality."[2] I wholeheartedly shared that vision when I took on the task of running the CHA.

"As CEO, Gene Jones is directly responsible for implementing the CHA's extensive redevelopment program of public housing, continuing the agency's mixed-income focus-strategic initiatives to help build strong, vibrant communities throughout Chicago," City Club of Chicago Board of Governors Chairman Edward Mazur said of my appointment. "Gene Jones brings more than 35 years of service and experience in housing operations, resident services, accounting and finance, auditing, maintenance, new construction, capital construction, housing choice, [and] voucher programs."[3]

"You don't get into something to test the waters," I told my staff, "You go into it to make waves. And that's what we're doing. We're making waves right now."

During one of my speaking engagements in Chicago, I told a group, "We must create an opportunity, 'within CHA'. This is what I want to talk about today—what it means for CHA, our residents, and the city of Chicago as a whole to create opportunities. All of us have a stake in CHA's mission—all of us in this room. You've no doubt heard about CHA. A lot of individuals have not heard about CHA. They don't know what we've done. They know what we've done in the past and reflect on all of the ugly things, but no one reflects on today and what we're trying to do in the future. And hopefully, I'm going to dispel some of those rumors, especially when I get to the reserves. Because it seems like everyone thinks I have this pot of money—I'm the leprechaun that has a pot of money, right?

Every housing authority in the country must have at least three months of operating reserves on hand at all times. That would mean CHA has at least $110 million. When I came to CHA they had $400 million in reserves. In a little less than a year and a half, I brought it down to $110 million. Reserves can be used for development, and that is what I did.

I told another group that the Chicago Housing Authority "looks much different today than it did in the 1990s and even 2000". Today, new mixed-income development includes a mix of renters and homeowners who live side-by-side and reflect the kind of economic diversity that every sustainable community should have, with new resources from new retail to parks and community centers that enhance the lives of residents. Our support for residents remains one of our biggest priorities and is helping people create their own opportunity.

"In 2017, we delivered and had in progress over 1,800 units of new Chicago housing. Our user project-based vouchers have allowed us to support affordable housing apartments all over the city. We brought 509 new affordable housing apartments using project-based vouchers. We have 708 project-based vouchers, units, and properties in 2018. What does this mean? Units are all over this city of Chicago. We have an investment in every one of our 77 community areas in the city of Chicago. This is a first for CHA, but we did not do it alone. CHA is a co-investor, meaning that there are others doing the work with us, and we need developers and all the community organizations to continue to identify opportunities for us.

"I'm reminded of a quote from Winston Churchill. 'A pessimist sees difficulty in every opportunity. An optimist sees opportunity in every difficulty.'"

In April of 2019, I had the privilege to speak to the Chicago City Club about youth education. I was excited to introduce Joushlyn Jones, who told her story about reaching her educational goals with CHA's help. She graduated from college with honors after receiving a POSSE Foundation scholarship. She told the group how the help she received served as a turning point in equipping her with the life skills that she carries with her today.[4]

"One of my most memorable experiences was participating in a CHA reading and math enrichment program sponsored by Siemens Technologies over the summer," she said. "That summer, I was not only introduced into the world of STEM, but I also was introduced to myself and my work ethic, a work ethic that I took back to school with me that fall. The Chicago Housing Authority introduced me to myself by giving me the gift of exposure. That exposure gave me hope, and that hope filled my ambition to basically write my own narrative."[5]

Joushlyn has since gone on to become a special education teacher at an elementary school on the south side of Chicago. There, she makes a difference in the lives of children from kindergarten through fourth grade. "While Joushlyn is exceptional, she is not the exception," I told the City Club. "We've helped many students like Joushlyn. The pathway out of poverty is through education, ladies and gentlemen, and the CHA impacts our youth and our adults. Four in ten CHA residents over 18 years old have pursued some form of post-secondary education, and over 7,500 residents in Chicago are in college. CHA adult residents have earned approximately 10,000 post-secondary degrees ranging from certificates to graduate degrees. Some have earned as high as PhDs, JDs and MDs."[6]

In March of 2019, with a mayoral election underway, rumors began swirling that I was leaving for a similar post in New York City. "I need to dispel a rumor," I told the City Club. "I've not interviewed for a job or talked to anyone about that. I have made a commitment to CHA, my residents, staff, and board."[7]

At the same City Club meeting in March of 2019, Mayor Emanuel lauded the work my staff and I had done for the city:

> "When you think about the fact that under [Gene's] stewardship and John Hooker's stewardship, we ended the 50-year federal oversight of our housing. And we are very close to completing the plan for transformation," the mayor said.[8]

> "Gene has taken the heart and interest of the residents to place and made sure that what they see in their neighborhood is like every other neighborhood, and they're not isolated from it and distant from it geographically, psychologically, and physically," Emanuel added. "And he has done an incredible job at re-inventing and re-imagining public housing in Chicago."[9]

In July 2019, CHA Board Chairman John T. Hooker announced his resignation after his four-year term expired. One month later, in August of 2019, I announced my resignation, intending to leave in September. The dual resignations allowed new mayor, Lori Lightfoot, to make her first appointment for a major department since beginning her term as the city's first black female mayor.[10]

I knew from experience that a new mayor always wants his or her people in key positions. Even before Mayor Emanuel announced his resignation, I knew that Mayor Lightfoot would not re-appoint Hooker. I had consistently told people if and when he left, I would leave as well. Another factor in my decision was being frozen out when the new mayor formed her own task force to look into the public housing issue. I guess you could say with that move, the writing was on the wall.

I had told the mayor I would stay through September, but a new city was courting me at the time, and the news soon leaked that I was going to Atlanta. Once the mayor found out I was leaving, she demanded my immediate resignation, which I gave her.

"Since my arrival at CHA four and a half years ago, I have been committed to meeting CHA's goals of producing more housing and to supporting the city in its efforts to expand housing opportunities in every Chicago community," I said in announcing my resignation.[11]

"From bringing new investment to communities and forming innovative partnerships that led to the development of three co-located housing and libraries, the development of new community assets like grocery stores and recreational facilities and the settlement earlier this year of the landmark Gautreaux case, I leave knowing that the CHA is well-positioned for the future and is prepared to meet the housing needs of its residents and the communities across our city," I concluded in my announcement.[12]

"He was a great leader. He had a great relationship with the residents," Alderman Pat Dowell chairman of the City Council's Budget Committee, said about me. "Every time you turned around, it was not unusual to see Gene at an event the residents were organizing; whether it was a summer picnic, the Christmas holiday party or Thanksgiving dinner, he was there."[13]

With the new mayor at the helm, I decided to leave immediately and head south. I was off to Atlanta, Georgia.

– Chapter 9 –

Heading to the ATL

I got a letter from a recruiting committee asking me if I wanted to go to Atlanta to work for their housing authority, nearing the end of my tenure in Chicago. They also wanted to know if I knew others who might be interested. I gave them five names, and they called me later to gauge my interest.

New York City was also looking for a new chairperson for their housing agency. They had a receiver, who met with the staff and the mayor. My name was floated as a possibility; although, they never formally contacted me. Instead, they picked a friend of mine, Greg Rusk, to head their agency. I was thoroughly happy with that decision, and for Greg as well.

Initially, I didn't want to go to Atlanta but ended up interviewing and learning what they needed. Ultimately, I accepted their offer. The Atlanta Housing Authority Board (AHA) hired me as its new president and CEO on September 10, 2019. I began work in early October. After leaving Chicago, I was ready for another challenge. Atlanta fit the bill of a city where I could help fix their public housing issues. I was thrilled by the response I got from city leaders.

"Gene is a proven leader in public housing and public finance, and the Board of Commissioners and staff welcome him to Atlanta with open arms," Atlanta Housing Board Chairman Christopher Edwards said. "He brings a wealth of knowledge and experience and will build upon the stability and clarity of purpose established under CEO Joy Fitzgerald."[1]

"We have deliberated on what we think is the most important thing that a board can do and that is to hire, and/or in some cases fire a CEO," Edwards said of my appointment. "That is a board's primary responsibility and, once that person is hired, then to support them and let them get on about the business of providing affordable housing."[2]

"I'd like to thank the AHA Board of Commissioners for their thorough, deliberate, and thoughtful selection progress," Mayor Keisha Lance Bottoms added. "[Jones] has shown dedication, expertise, and effectiveness in creating affordable housing in major cities across North America. He will be a valued leader in helping bring to fruition our One Atlanta Housing Affordability Action Plan."[3]

Shortly after beginning my tenure in Atlanta, I wrote an open letter to the community:

It is with great excitement that I bring you greetings as the new president and CEO of Atlanta Housing. I am happy and proud of this opportunity to lead the largest public housing agency in the state of Georgia and one of the most innovative in the entire nation. Our job at Atlanta Housing is all about you. You are at the very center of our efforts to preserve affordable housing, because we believe everyone should be able to live, work, and thrive in healthy, amenity-rich environments that offer access to transportation, jobs, and great schools, and provides resources such as job training, programs for our youth, and services for our seniors.

Stable housing is the foundation of success, and affordable housing is not just important for those we serve. It positively impacts our communities and our society both economically and socially, so it is important for us all. As I settle in to my new city and my new position, I will keep at the forefront of my thoughts Atlanta Housing's need to continue partnerships and efforts that not only house our residents but also support our residents through human development services. This kind of support is critical, because it helps to spur economic and educational growth and encourages our seniors to live fuller lives as they age in place.

Our approach is intentionally holistic, because we understand that people are the heartbeat of communities, not buildings. We are all better, and so are our communities, when everyone has the opportunity to succeed. This edition of the newly revamped Home Front publication renews our commitment to keeping our residents better informed about agency and residential happenings. Each issue will include greetings from me, resident highlights, and agency updates. We hope you enjoy it. Saying goodbye to summer is simply an opportunity to say hello to fall. As I close one chapter of my life, I look forward to saying hello to something wonderful and new. Change is inevitable. This change is definitely good!

Respectfully, Eugene Jones, Jr.

Just a few months before I came on board, Mayor Bottoms had announced the city's first-ever affordable housing action plan. Her plan included investing $1 billion in combined public and private funds to combat rising housing costs and the displacement of longtime residents. It fulfilled a campaign promise she had made when running for mayor.

The *Atlanta Journal-Constitution* described the mayor's plan as offering "a menu of policy proposals. They range from finding ways to use existing public dollars and land as an incentive to attract private sector investment to changes in zoning, expediting redevelopment of vacant and blighted properties, developer incentives, and the creation of a housing innovation lab."[4]

The goal of the mayor's ambitious plan was to substantially increase the number of Atlanta residents who could afford housing. It included collaboration among multiple city agencies as well as a diverse group of nonprofits. Included in the mix were philanthropic and faith-based organizations, educational institutions, private companies, residents, and community members. All were covered under the "House ATL" banner to meet the housing needs of Atlanta residents.

"We have a good vision. We have a good board," I told the *Atlanta Voice*. "Everyone is looking at Atlanta Housing to do some innovative things, but we also need partners in order to accomplish that. What we're trying to do at Atlanta Housing is to just keep forward in building affordable housing, making sure that we build communities and not just bricks and mortar. With the partnerships we have in place now, determining how we expound on that and get more people to the table is going to be a great feat for Atlanta Housing."[5]

"We look forward to incorporating what the mayor is looking for in regard to affordable housing, that we can do it in this city faster, being very innovative but with more partners," I told the *Voice*.[6]

As I assumed my new role, I had the privilege of working in transition with interim CEO Joy Fitzgerald. She took over in late April 2019 after Gregory Johnson, AHA's original choice to lead the agency, decided to remain as the CEO of Cincinnati's housing agency.

One of the first things I had to tackle was a long-standing legal dispute between the AHA and former CEO Renee Glover. She claimed in a 2018 lawsuit that the City of Atlanta had smeared her. The city alleged Glover facilitated so-called "sweetheart" land deals with the Integral Group real estate developer. The board authorized me to settle all claims with Glover so we could move on with other issues facing the city. One of the city's business writers thanked me for "heralding in a new day at Atlanta Housing."

"Let's put this sordid chapter behind us and get to the business of building and developing more affordable homes for people with limited means," Maria Saporta wrote in *The Saporta Report*. "I'm grateful we once again have an innovative leader at the housing authority who can help Atlanta reclaim its place as a leader in housing policies."[7]

I quickly learned that I inherited a great staff who wanted to do the right thing for the city and help those in need. "We can't do housing for everyone," I told a radio interviewer after I had been on the job about one month, "but we can provide the opportunity for housing for everyone in Atlanta through our partnerships with other entities and taking a holistic approach."[8]

The Housing Authority also tackled the issue of affordability and Section 8 housing, which I addressed in a November 2019 interview with National Public Radio's WABE.

"You have the working poor that needs to be addressed. You have the low-income folks that need to be addressed," I told interviewer Jim Burress. "As you know, wages have not escalated like the cost of housing. It's sad to say that everyone wants to make money: these developers, these landowners, and these builders, and so forth. But someone's got to have compassion."[9]

We also looked to do more than just buildings. As I told the *Atlanta Voice*, the housing authority also got involved in other support services and partnerships between the public and private sectors. We also wanted to build houses that fit into the neighborhoods.

"We will not build 100-percent affordable housing anymore," I told the *Voice*. "What we will build is mixed-income developments that fit into a neighborhood that you will see that is seamless. You wouldn't know if there was a public housing or a subsidized resident there, or a market rate over there. We're trying to incorporate neighborhood values in these neighborhoods that we are a part of."[10]

Part of my job in Atlanta was meeting with and speaking to community groups. One of those opportunities came in February 2020, when I spoke at the Transform Westside Summit. Having lived in colder climates for a large part of my life, I was surprised that people in Atlanta actually made it out of the house in 30-degree weather. "You all don't do good in the cold," I told the crowd to their laughter. "You darn sure don't do good in snow."

After telling the audience about some of my experiences in other communities, I reiterated my passion for HUD's Section 3. That program requires:

> *That recipients of certain HUD financial assistance provide training, employment, contracting and other economic opportunities to low- and very low-income persons, especially recipients of government assistance for housing, and to businesses that provide economic opportunities to low- and very low-income person.*[11]

"When I was in Chicago, I took it to another level. I put it on steroids," I told the crowd. "What happened was we had an opportunity to really prove that we were dedicated for employment and also building businesses who were Section 3, who deserved it and could get work from Chicago Housing Authority. I established a program called the Jobs Program the second year I started, and I created a Section 3 office that no one has across this country."[12]

I also assured supporters and critics that they would eventually see the benefits of investing in Section 3.

"Just wait on it because it's going to come, and it's going to be very beneficial. You're going to be very happy with the programs we come out with at Atlanta Housing."

I concluded my remarks by discussing the realities everyday Americans face because of the lack of affordable housing. "Housing costs are off the chain," I told them. "Families are forced to cut back on the basic necessities such as food, healthcare, and clothing, and that's what's not being addressed in America, in my opinion."

"The homeless population is not going to go away because we're not doing it correctly. Everyone is piecemealing it. Everyone's doing great things, but we're not doing anything holistically… because we need all our resources all together with people who do this every day and figure it out. That's the only way we're going to combat homelessness, and that's the only way we're going to combat affordable housing."[13]

Unfortunately, politics again raised its ugly head over the settlement I negotiated in the legal dispute between the AHA and former CEO Renee Glover. It came before the AHA board the day after my presentation at the Transform Westside Summit. They rejected the settlement I had negotiated, opting to continue litigation against the Integral Group and its development partners.

Because these lawsuits had cost AHA and the city millions of dollars in legal fees, one of my first goals was to settle these matters. Under the previous mayor, building affordable housing in Atlanta had come to a standstill because of the legal disputes.

Less than a week later, the AHA board of commissioners unanimously approved the same settlement agreement they had refused to vote on the previous week. By doing so, they hopefully averted a trial in the long legal battle. The board's change of heart came after protracted negotiations that one party said included concessions agreed to by the Integral Group.[14]

Such is the role politics often plays in public housing. It's part of the game, and something I've dealt with my entire career in helping provide affordable public housing to those in need.

In Atlanta, we also faced the challenge of preserving affordability. One of our strategies at the housing authority was purchasing land or buildings to promote stability in the community.

"What we did in Chicago is we bought buildings that made sense and were appropriate based on our mission," I told a reporter from the *Washington Post*. "I'm not saying that Atlanta Housing is going to buy every building that comes up for sale in Atlanta, but those are some options to preserve affordable housing."

I also stressed that while creating new affordable housing is important, maintaining what's already there is also crucial. "You've got to maintain what you have," I told the *Post*. "It's so hard to build new; you've got to maintain what you have."[15]

Some politicians were also paying attention to what was happening in public housing. As a result, I was summoned to Washington D.C., to appear before the House Financial Services Committee subcommittee.

Several other housing experts and I were asked to provide insights on how to and why it is essential to protect public housing programs. Financial Services Committee Chairwoman Representative Maxine Waters (D-CA), along with Senator Kamala Harris (D-CA), had introduced a bill seeking more than $100 billion in investment for affordable housing. They claimed the legislation was needed to counter the Trump Administration's efforts to defund affordable housing programs. Sidestepping the politics, I began my testimony:

> It is this body of experience that informs my remarks today," I told the subcommittee. "I have seen all sides of the coin— what happens when there is full investment in public housing, what happens when there is not, and what happens when you view public housing as an asset, and what happens when it is seen as a warehouse or worse, as a blight.
>
> Given these questions both in terms of impact on individuals and on communities, while I will reference a variety of communities and experiences, there is no question that Chicago's public housing [authority] presents the most complete case study of the building, the fall, and the resurrection of public housing, its residents, and the communities in which they live.

I'm going to take a different tact [than] my colleagues because I agree with most cases about the lack of funding and so forth over all these years, these three decades, the lack of funding. However, it takes a different view of how to manage, how to create, how to keep the housing that you have existing based on limited resources. It provides a way in which you have to use your skill set in order to work public-private partnerships to make the best of a maybe bad situation.

I have been blessed, or I have been lucky to work at a variety of housing authorities that have funding mechanisms [in which] I can create, and that I can maintain and acquire housing. As I've always said across this country, I think every housing authority should be an MTW—which is Moving to Work—because it provides flexibility for my colleagues.

It is important for the smaller housing authorities, as well as the medium size and the large, too—to anticipate, to direct, to assist in these public-private partnerships for flexibility in the funding that they get from HUD. It comes in a bundle, you have fungibility, and you can provide the same amount of housing, but you can leverage those dollars and create better housing. And also, with MTW agencies, you can provide the opportunity where you can be innovative.

In Chicago, we did three libraries which had public housing above the library, providing a benefit for the whole community. Those were a resounding success because we were able to be very innovative by using the state resources, using the city resources, and using the HUD resources we received. These, along with all the other public-private partnership and philanthropic agencies, demonstrated we can pool our resources and come up with a strategy that's best for a community.

I think if we work much better with other agencies like the VA, Transportation, and HHS—because we're all in this together—is how we can meld together different aspects of what we're providing with housing, transportation, education and health. So, how can we manage that with a holistic approach and provide a better housing situation for our communities? Let us not forget that we're here as executive directors, CEOs, everyone who's on this panel, we are trying to protect the residents' rights, we're trying to protect the residents' wellbeing and their quality of life.

I think, with the resources that we do have, I think they're limited. But I think that with the resources we do have that we can manage those resources the best that we can and get the best product for our residents.[16]

In March 2020, we also dealt with the COVID-19 (Coronavirus) outbreak and its impact on the housing community. Because many workers had either been furloughed or asked to work from home, most of the Atlanta Housing complexes were more crowded than usual during business hours. It made the challenge of "social distancing" even harder than before.

As a result, we were forced to cancel or postpone residential meetings. We had to invest in a thorough deep-cleaning of surfaces in common areas, and revise our service request protocols. One community went so far as to order a two-month stock of cleaning supplies for use in public areas like leasing offices, lobbies, and TV dens.

In April of 2020, Mayor Keisha Bottoms and I announced a program to help some residents struggling financially during the coronavirus pandemic. The program was designed to help seniors, families, and others who live in Atlanta Housing owned or subsidized units who have lost income due to the COVID-19 pandemic. Residents were eligible to receive rent reduction for up to two months, with AHA making payments directly to the property owner or management company. Some eligible residents could have their entire months' rent covered under the program.[17]

"Atlanta Housing's rent relief efforts are designed to address the financial uncertainty residents face due to the pandemic and subsequent shelter-in-place order," AHA Board Chair Dr. Christopher Edwards said in announcing the measures.[18]

As I write this, the City of Atlanta, the United States, and the world are still dealing with the repercussions of the COVID-19 pandemic.

The most significant impact of COVID-19 in Atlanta has been managing the office differently than before. Many of my 350 employees have been telecommuting and won't be returning to the office. We are still able to provide the same services with fewer people in the office. My primary responsibility is to protect the staff and the residents.

Moving forward, I think we will see a ripple effect from the pandemic. Many businesses will discover they don't need thousands of feet of office space. Among other areas of the economy, the after-effects of COVID-19 will ripple through commercial real estate affecting utility companies, restaurants, and many other businesses.

— II —

My Call-to-Action: Reforming National Housing Policy

We need leaders who recognize the harm being done to people and planet through the dominant practices that control, ignore, abuse, and oppress the human spirit.
We need leaders who put service over self, stand steadfast in crises and failures, and who display unshakable faith that people can be generous, creative, and kind.
Margaret Wheatley

– Chapter 10 –

National Housing Vision

The concept of shelter-in-place has been part of our national fight against COVID-19 since early in 2020. It had been hoped that many Americans would limit unnecessary exposure to others by staying at home, thus limiting the spread of the disease.

This is fine, provided you *have* a safe home in which to seek shelter, safety, and comfort.

Current estimates suggest that between 10 to 15 percent of Americans have housing insecurity. This may mean their rent is too high for their income, their home is unsafe or overcrowded, or they are homeless. Housing insecurity for some of our most vulnerable citizens is a reality. And yet, the issue of affordable housing in America has not received the coverage it and Americans deserve.

I have spent my entire career working for public housing agencies in cities like Atlanta, Chicago, Toronto, New Orleans, and Detroit. I have learned that there are solutions to the housing crisis in America. But we can't even begin to fix these problems until we first free ourselves from the lingo that has become all too commonplace. This includes phrases such as affordable housing, public housing, projects, etc.

These words create an us-versus-them mentality.

Ask the average American what public housing means to them, and they will probably describe some variation of a ghetto. That is an unsafe and unlovely place where people go because they have nowhere else to lay their heads.

We don't need *public* housing in America. We need housing. Full stop. Plain English. *Housing.*

Affordable housing is another common term that we bandy about all the time as a common refrain! America needs more affordable housing. And that statement is not wrong. Not exactly. But what is affordable? Is affordable housing in urban Atlanta the same thing as in rural Montana? Do the wealthy have the same perception of *affordability* as middle class or low-income Americans? Of course not. That is because affordable housing means different things to different people in different parts of the county.

We don't need affordable housing in America. We need housing.

We need housing that all Americans can afford.

We need housing all Americans can afford and is supported by public agencies across our nation.

Instead of affordable housing, why not call it, "adjustable community housing"?

In my 35 years of working in the public housing sector, I've been nicknamed Mr. Fix-It because that is what I do. I am brought in when things are already sliding downhill. It's my job to lend my experience and skills to troubled housing agencies. Most of the time, these agencies face financial challenges and a host of other problems that have impacted their ability to provide effectively and economically what people need—safe housing.

Americans do not just need a roof over their head. They need safe homes where they can settle down and settle in. Homes where they can grow roots. Places they are proud to call home. Not just a box in a skyrise, but a home that is part of a broader community.

They need to have pride in a place.

They need strong communities.

I think we suffer from a narrow perspective when it comes to our housing crisis, nationally and at a state level. It is not just about housing, but about so much more. It is about the neighborhood, the community, and the services within that community.

We need to create places where all people can be proud to live. Areas with easy access to groceries, healthcare, and schools. Safe places with greenspace and libraries that are welcoming to all. We are not looking to build warehouses for our most vulnerable citizens.

We owe them, and our nation, so much more.

I have a vision for addressing the nation's housing challenges, much like I have done in every city I've served over the last three-plus decades.

My vision involves resident-focused customer service.

My vision is honest oversight to combat fraud.

My vision is for comprehensive community services.

My vision is humanizing leadership and project design.

My vision is not about changing a *specific* housing authority, but about bringing the spirit and the framework for creating community social change that is meaningful and endures.

Those of us in positions of power must recognize *social housing* is a customer-service oriented industry. The residents of every neighborhood across the United States deserve a voice in their living opportunities. We are not just building houses; we are building communities.

And how might adjustable community housing look over the next decade in the United States?

A little differently, I believe, depending on where you are in the country and whether your neighborhood is urban, rural, or suburban. But not *so* different.

We all want durable roofs over our heads, green spaces to explore, access to affordable food and transportation, and good schools for our children.

We all want our governments and our leaders to be honest, wise, and accountable.

We all want programs and services which enrich our bodies, minds, souls, and communities.

And we all want leaders who share our vision and who possess the skills and enthusiasm to help us realize our dreams.

Housing needs to return to our national agenda.

Housing needs to become a realizable dream. I believe creating nationwide adjustable community housing will help us build strong neighborhoods and communities we all, as Americans, can take pride in.

Won't you join me in this crusade? Together, we can build communities where people can live in dignity and safety and become contributors to society as we move ahead into the future.

– Chapter 11–

Proof is in the Problem

America's national housing system is broken. It is not because there are so many individual housing programs in need of repair. The system, instead, is broken primarily because of grossly inadequate funding for some of these programs; because of poor federal management and administration of fundamental aspects of national housing policy; and because some essential programs require new legislation so they can have the impact that was intended.

The evidence for a revamped, reformed national housing policy is abundantly clear, and the proof is in the *problem*, in its vast scale and scope. It seems we have been grappling with one crisis after another. Even before the COVID-19 crisis induced potential mass eviction and homelessness crises, America was already burdened with an affordable housing crisis.

Now, with COVID having pushed unemployment to levels unseen since the Great Depression, our nation may be flirting with perhaps unprecedented social and economic disasters. This will especially be the case, if, as some epidemiologists fear, the upcoming fall and winter months induce another surge of COVID infections that necessitate a second national shutdown.

The specific facts and data points that illustrate our housing crises are truly sobering:

71

There are just 7.2 million affordable and available rental homes for the nation's 11.2 million extremely low-income renters.[1] "Only 36 affordable and available rental homes exist for every 100 extremely low-income renter households," according to the National Low-Income Housing Coalition.[2]

And "extremely low-income renters face a shortage in every state and major metropolitan area, including the District of Columbia. Among states, the supply of affordable and available rental homes ranges from only 18 for every 100 extremely low-income renter households in Nevada to 62 in West Virginia."[3]

It is estimated that 10 to 15 percent of Americans suffer from housing insecurity.[4]

Three out of four American households eligible for U.S. Department of Housing & Urban Development (HUD) housing aid fail to receive it because of inadequate HUD funding.[5]

A 2016 national survey reported that 53-percent of waiting lists for the largest federal housing assistance program—Housing Choice Voucher program—were not accepting new applicants. It's unlikely that this situation has noticeably improved.[6]

Data from 2019 shows that 42-percent of public housing properties finished their last construction before 1975—and they represent 51-percent of public housing units.[7]

Just 22-percent of public housing properties (representing 17 percent of units) have undergone construction since 1997.[8]

The NAHB/Wells Fargo Housing Opportunity Index (HOI), which measures the extent of housing affordability in America reached an 8-month low in August 2020, due to increased housing prices and supply chain impediments brought on by COVID.[9]

A June 2020 national survey by the National Housing Law Project of 100 legal aid and civil rights attorneys reported that over 90-percent respondents had reported illegal evictions in their area.[10]

And certainly, most alarmingly, absent national action, after COVID-induced evictions moratoriums across the nation expire, as many as 40 million Americans could lose their homes by year end, according to the Aspen Institute. Forty million Americans exceeds the entire population of Canada.[11]

The Trump Administration has never afforded the affordable housing crisis or national housing policy the priority it deserves.

Like clockwork, every year President Trump has proposed substantial reductions in HUD programs targeting people in need. Just this year, Trump's proposed budget to Congress again included draconian cuts in HUD funding—a massive $9.6 billion reduction. Fortunately, for low-income people, Congress has mostly turned a deaf ear to Trump's requested cuts, but Trump's administration has found other ways to hinder efforts to ensure fair access to affordable housing for low-income Americans.[12]

The Trump HUD Department announced, in July 2020, that it will be ending the Obama Administration rule that requires cities and towns that receive federal housing funds to assess local housing patterns for racial bias and to develop plans to address such identifiable bias.[13]

The National Association of Realtors, hardly a bastion of rabid liberalism, sharply criticized the Trump HUD Department's action because it "significantly weakens the federal government's commitment to the goals of the Fair Housing Act."[14]

A Brief History of National Housing Policy

For the newcomer to federal housing policy, a brief review of its history and a thumbnail sketch of current programs may be helpful. The birth of federal housing assistance, as we know it today, was in 1935, as part of President Franklin Roosevelt's New Deal program. Under the National Industrial Recovery Act, enacted in June 1933, Roosevelt's new Public Works Administration (PWA) was instructed to support the development of "construction, reconstruction, alteration, or repair of low-cost housing and slum clearance projects."[15]

Also, in 1934, the PWA's Housing Division began the direct construction of public housing, and by 1937, it had built fifty-two housing projects throughout the U.S.[16]

Additionally in 1937, the enactment of the Wagner-Steagall National Housing Act created the Federal Housing Administration (FHA) to provide mortgage insurance on loans made by FHA-approved lenders. Another New Deal-era milestone, the Housing Act of 1937 established the United States Housing Authority to help develop slum-clearance projects and construct low-rent housing.[17]

A major accomplishment of FDR's successor, Harry Truman and his Fair Deal, was the passage of the American Housing Act of 1949, which significantly broadened FHA mortgage insurance authority and increased public housing expenditures to construct 810,000 new units.[18]

A landmark of President Lyndon Johnson's Great Society was the passage of Housing and Urban Development Act of 1965. Johnson described the Act as the "'single most important breakthrough in federal housing policy' since the 1920s." The Act substantially expanded federal housing expenditures, and, among other provisions, funded rent subsidies for the elderly and disabled. Under the Act, the Department of Housing and Urban Development was established as a cabinet-level agency.[19]

Another legislative milestone to note in our short tour of the history of federal housing policy is the Housing and Community Development Act of 1974. It created the Section 8 housing voucher program, now called the Housing Choice Voucher Program, to help low-income people pay for affordable homes in the private market, with most tenants required to pay no more that *30-percent* of their income for rent, with federal subsidies accounting for the remaining costs.[20]

This program is now HUD's largest funded program. HUD's programs today largely encompass three distinct areas. The first being public housing in which housing properties for low-income people are financed by the federal government and owned and operated by local housing authorities. Second are project-based rental assistance programs where contracts are made with private property owners to fund housing assistance that provides units for low-income households. The third type is the aforementioned Housing Choice Voucher Program, which assists about 2.3 million low-income households.[22]

Benefits of National Housing Assistance

An abundance of evidence demonstrates that existing housing assistance programs provide low-income people a range of indirect benefits in addition to the direct benefits of living in affordable, stable housing. It was estimated, for example, that housing subsidies lifted 2.9 million people out of poverty in 2017.[22]

The lack of housing instability can inflict a host of harmful health problems on people, as noted in a 2018 Project Hope report that surveyed the healthcare literature. The report stated:

People who are not chronically homeless but face housing instability (in the form of moving frequently, falling behind on rent, or couch surfing) are more likely to experience poor health in comparison to their stably housed peers. Residential instability is associated with health problems among youth, including increased risks of teen pregnancy, early drug use, and depression. A review of twenty-five studies that examined the impact of foreclosure on mental health and health behaviors (including substance abuse) found that all of the studies reported that foreclosure was associated with worsened outcomes, including depression, anxiety, increased alcohol use, psychological distress, and suicide.[23]

A 2018 study published in the *Journal of Health and Social Behavior* concluded that "[h]ousing assistance policies may lead to improved mental health for children and adolescents by improving housing quality, stability, and affordability." The study used "a unique data linkage of the National Health Interview Survey and U.S. Department of Housing and Urban Development administrative data to examine the impact of housing assistance on parent-reported mental health outcomes for children ages 2 to 17."[24]

Interestingly, the study found "that children living in public housing have better mental health outcomes," but it "did not find similar benefits" for children whose families were receiving housing vouchers.[25]

A broader focused health and housing analysis, the Public and Affordable Housing Research Corporation (PAHRC) 2019 Housing Impact Report, found that that housing assistance programs improve the state of health for the of many low-income families:

> *The housing stability provided by publicly supported housing programs can translate into improved health outcomes for some of our nation's most vulnerable families. Publicly supported homes can enable families to spend more money on healthcare, improve the quality of their residence, and reduce their exposure to stress caused by housing instability, all of which can lead to positive health outcomes. For instance, access to publicly supported homes can reduce exposure to home health hazards, including lead-based paint and overcrowded living conditions. Some health researchers consider a quality affordable home to be a vaccine, or safeguard, that can protect families against long-term health problems and support healthy lifestyles.*[26]

A 2018 Urban Institute study reached similar conclusions:

Housing quality and location directly affects a person's health from before birth through his or her advanced years. Evidence from the Moving to Opportunity demonstration, which provided public housing families with vouchers they could only use in low-poverty areas, showed significant health benefits for women and girls, including lower levels of obesity, diabetes, and depression.[27]

The PAHRC report also addresses how government housing agencies can even find ways to boost the educational performance of low-income children:

[E]xpanding access to affordable homes near good school districts can play an important role in connecting low-income and minority families to better schools. This can significantly reduce the achievement gap between these children and their higher-income peers. Publicly supported rental housing can also connect children to valuable educational services. For example, Denver Housing Authority's (CO) Bridge Program offers literacy training, academic support, and social learning programs for children after school. Children participating in the Bridge Program were less likely to be disciplined in school, had higher rates of school attendance, and received greater teacher ratings of proficiency for math and science compared to low-income children living in similar neighborhoods without a structured after-school program.[28]

The Urban Institute report once again echoed the PAHRC report: "Housing stability also affects educational outcomes for children, such as how frequently they change schools or are absent from class and their ability to learn in class, complete homework, and score well on tests."[29]

The PAHRC report identified the economic gains resulting from housing assistance:

Publicly supported homes play an important role in stimulating the local economy by creating jobs, boosting children's earnings in adulthood, and increasing the size of the family's discretionary income that can be spent on goods and services beyond housing. If all the cost-burdened, low-income renter households received rental assistance in 2015, disposable income available for necessities like food and healthcare would increase $321 per month on average, representing a $48.8 billion investment in the sustainability of low-income families.[30]

Precisely because housing aid programs can and do deliver a spectrum of societal benefits only reinforces the need for comprehensive housing policy reform. One might argue if such programs are working by providing benefits, how can housing policy be broken? However, national housing policy, to a large extent, is nonetheless broken because several of these programs are unable to scale sufficiently to meet the vast needs still unmet.

That is because they often lack the adequate resources, the administrative flexibility, or in some cases, the adequate legislative authority. That is a manifest failure of overall national housing policy, not of the various programs themselves.

– Chapter 12–

A Holistic Approach to Housing

More than ever before, America urgently needs comprehensive housing reform—sustainable over time and generations that will materially improve the lot of lower income people whose needs are now unmet while also bettering the communities in which they live. The last point is especially important.

If we are to significantly improve housing for those most in need, we must also improve the communities where the housing exists; or put another way, if we are to significantly improve communities most in need, we must significantly improve the housing in those communities. Housing must be viewed as a nucleus for all national anti-poverty efforts as it's so interrelated with all aspects of anti-poverty policy.

Guiding Principles for National Housing Reform

With that as a preamble, there are three overarching principles I think should guide our nation's housing policy reform work: 1) greater public and private resources with increased local empowerment; 2) a more holistic approach to public policy and 3) the prioritization of resident-focused strategies.

I will examine each one separately.

1) Greater public and private resources; increased local empowerment

Comprehensive national housing reform will certainly demand greater federal funding and more private capital; but, it also will require a concerted effort to empower local housing authorities with increased flexibility to move quicker, as the problems cannot wait, and more creativelyzz to better match their programs with local need. Put more colorfully, they need more green and less red (i.e., tape).

Some have estimated Congress "must provide no less than $100 billion to ensure housing stability for the lowest-income renters during and after the pandemic." The problem does not simply necessitate more spending, *but better* spending. That also means reducing red tape so as to reduce the time it takes to complete housing developments, as less time taken can usually mean less money expended. It also necessitates some consolidation of the number of federally funded local public housing authorities. As each matter is of critical importance, each will be addressed separately ahead.

How much increase in annual budgetary authority does the U.S. Department of Housing and Urban Development (HUD) actually need to better address the growing housing needs nationwide? I would roughly estimate an additional $20 billion, with $10 billion of that carved out specifically for New York City, as their needs are so enormous.

Fortunately, as noted, there are several existing HUD-supported programs that could clearly benefit from an infusion of increased monies and capital, from both the public and private sectors, as well new supportive legislative actions. They include:

a.) Housing Choice Voucher Program
Former Vice President Biden and others have proposed making this program universally available, as it only serves about 25-percent of eligible people. Unfortunately, many low-income persons find

landlords unwilling to accept Section 8 vouchers. Some states have passed laws prohibiting such "source of income" discrimination; as most states have not, we need federal legislation to do the same nationwide.

b.) Section 3 of the 1968 HUD Act
Section 3 of the 1968 HUD Act is intended to encourage training, employment, contracting, and other economic opportunities for low-income people, and every public housing authority should be required to implement a complete Section 3 plan, as many do not today.

In Chicago, we focused on providing grants for Chicago Housing Authority residents to help them land jobs or start businesses. Our Section 3 program was on steroids—because we had a commitment on Section 3 to get our residents employed, to uplift them, and to get them out of public and assisted housing. That was the main thrust, and to build their businesses so they could bring on residents that lived in public and assisted housing in the surrounding community. I pride myself on this work.

And this is an approach that should be emulated by all distressed communities that receive HUD funding.

c.) Moving to Work
HUD's Moving to Work initiative, established in 1996, helps housing residents find employment and become self-sufficient, while allowing housing authorities to adopt innovative, locally crafted strategies that harness federal monies more efficiently—but just 39 of the 3,400 public housing authorities are signed on to the program.

d.) Low Income Housing Tax Credits
The Low Income Housing Tax Credit (LIHTC) program provides dollar-for-dollar federal tax credits to subsidize the acquisition, construction, and rehabilitation of affordable rental housing for low- and moderate-income tenants. Two types of tax credits, a 9-percent tax credit and a 4-percent tax credit, are offered. Both are designed to generate newly constructed, rehabbed, or refinanced rental

properties conforming to the same income eligibility standards and affordability requirements, but the 9-percent credit is clearly the preferable option for spurring low-income rental housing.

The program is overseen by state housing finance agencies with each state granted a fixed allocation of credits based on its population. The program has induced the construction or rehabilitation of about 110,000 affordable rental units each year since the mid-1990s.

Opportunity Zones

Opportunity zones are designed to spur private investment into low-income neighborhoods through a federal tax incentive. The program was created by Congress in 2017. About 8,700 opportunity zones have been designated across all 50 states for the next 10 years. In Chicago, the following criteria is used to identify communities eligible for opportunity zones: an unemployment rate of 20-percent or more; median family income of less than $38,000, which is approximately 50-percent of area median income, and a poverty rate of 30-percent or more.

Rental Assistance Demonstration (RAD)

The Rental Assistance Demonstration (RAD) program does not require congressional appropriations. Established during the Obama Administration, it is an innovative approach to allow public housing authorities to utilize public and private debt and equity for public housing building enhancements and repairs. As HUD notes, "the backlog of public housing capital needs is estimated at over $35 billion." I do think that the parameters in the RAD program are impressive, and that all local housing authorities should seriously examine the program. They should look at it in a way in which they fully understand the program, the potential outcomes, and end results.

New Markets Tax Credit

The New Markets Tax Credit (NMTC) program channels private capital into low-income communities by allowing individual and corporate investors to receive a tax credit against their federal income tax in exchange for making equity investments in these communities. According to the New Markets Tax Credits Coalition, "between 2003 and Sept. 2019, $52 billion in direct NMTC investments were made in businesses and these NMTC investments leveraged more than $100 billion in total capital investment to businesses and revitalization projects in communities with high rates of poverty and unemployment."[1]

Federal Historic Tax Incentives Preservation
The federal preservation tax incentives program fosters private investments in the rehabilitation of historic buildings. Since 1976, it has attracted over $100 billion in private dollars to preserve over 45,000 historic buildings—with many in lower income communities badly in need of such rehabilitation.

The tax program, as described by the National Park Service, "has revived, abandoned, or underutilized schools, warehouses, factories, churches, retail stores, apartments, hotels, houses, agricultural buildings, offices, and other buildings across the country, and in turn, has helped support the redevelopment of entire downtowns and neighborhoods."[2]

Consolidation of Local Public Housing Agencies
Astonishingly, the U.S. Department of Housing and Urban Development (HUD) does not require regular impact reports from the 3,400 public housing agencies (PHAs) it oversees. Not only must that change, but the very existence of some of these 3,400 agencies should also be a reform target. Public housing agencies are not post offices. There is, demonstrably, room for consolidation of some of these agencies to generate potential economies of scale and cost savings.

A 2016 study from the nonpartisan Center on Budget and Policy Priorities, "Consolidating Rental Assistance Would Increase Efficiency and Expand Opportunity," declared:

The large number of program administrators and the small number of households that many of them assist increase administrative costs and reduce rental assistance programs' effectiveness. The number of agencies also can hinder eligible families' ability to use rental vouchers to live where they choose, including in safer neighborhoods that have better schools and access to jobs or other services but that are located in another housing agency's jurisdiction. Despite the potential benefits of consolidation to achieve economies of scale and facilitate administration of rental assistance throughout a metropolitan area, few PHAs have voluntarily merged with others.[3]

The study also observed that "[d]espite the potential benefits of consolidation to achieve economies of scale and facilitate administration of rental assistance throughout a metropolitan area, few PHAs have voluntarily merged with others."[4]

It recommended that the "[a]dministration should act promptly to finalize a proposed rule change to allow PHAs that form a consortium to have a single funding contract for Housing Choice Vouchers, and to revise the voucher administrative fee policy to remove the financial disincentive for small PHAs to enter into consortia or otherwise consolidate."[5]

1.) Reducing Red Tape

I have particularly strong feelings on this issue as they are born from my direct experience from the many years of frustration trying to navigate through reams of federal red tape to get housing development projects solidly off the ground. I discuss this issue in this section that addresses the need for greater public and private housing resources, because reducing the time and effort it takes to launch housing assistance projects can save public money—time is indeed money—which can thus free up limited funds for other housing programs.

Recently, someone asked me to elaborate on the problems associated with red tape in HUD programs and on what can be done to surmount it. With only limited editing, my response is below:

"If you look at Canada, Canada has no HUD. They also build based on design, land values, and so forth. They build it. They go straight to the board in a social housing entity, they approve it, then they build. There's no regulatory agency over there other than the city assuring that the dollars that they provide to the social housing gets spent in the right way and appropriately.

I am not saying HUD's internal mechanisms are to blame, but I am saying all of the 'red tape' is." It takes us five to ten years to get a development going. It's not because of HUD. It's because of the federal requirements for us to get to from point A to point B. And it's exhausting. Community involvement, zoning issues, permitting issues, regulatory issues, it's just so difficult. You have to know every stretch of the imagination when it comes to a new development and building affordable housing.

Even rehab of housing is very difficult to do from a housing authority's standpoint because of all the red tape. Environmental issues? Yes, we've got to do the environmental work. We've got to get them done quickly. You don't know if the city's going to do it or do you have to partner with someone else to do it. It's always about resources and availability of competent people from HUD's side, from the housing authority's side, from the city's side, and from the state's side. They all have to come together. There's no other housing agency that has to bring in all these partnerships and dot all their i's and cross all their t's like a public housing agency has to do.

It's a daunting task. Because you have to get outside resources, outside council, we have to have in-house counsel. And all that money's being paid because of the complexity of doing these deals.

You know, a private developer can say, "Okay, I want that piece of land over there and I'm going to build 3,000 units. Go into the city, go into the zone and get a pass and so forth, put my equity together, go to the bank, get my construction loan." Boom, it's done.

We, on the other hand, it takes us five to ten years. We have to get the land; we have to do a disposition application. We have to get HUD to approve that. Once the disposition application gets done, then we have to go back. We have to get the community involved. We have to make sure the city's on board. We've got to see what kind of funds we can leverage. Now, we've got to go to the state. We've got to apply for tax credits—either 9-percent or 4-percent. Hopefully, you'll get 9-percent. Because you don't have to do any gap findings and so forth.

Now, you've got to go to the bank. You've got to sell those tax credits. You've got to understand the syndication. You've got to get a bank involved. You have to get so many things. Banks fall out. They come back. You've got to re-do everything all over again. The paperwork, the paperwork, the paperwork. It's a belaboring task that I don't see any end unless someone cuts through that red tape.

I'm not trying to circumvent safety and environmental issues and so forth, but there's got to be something done that we can make it a quicker process and so forth and include everyone that we should be including in being transparent.

Well, I think they should look at legislation that the former mayor of Indianapolis, Stephen Goldsmith, and I put together, in 1998, called Home Rule. If someone goes back and looks at a Home Rule in 1998, what we tried to do is we tried to pool all our resources to the state, to the city in order to leverage the dollars so that we can build efficiently.

That means a housing authority would have CDBG in home funds under their umbrella so that they could leverage those dollars so that we have an overall goal—not a city goal, a housing authority goal, and a state goal.

Someone needs to look at that and see if that's feasible today to cut through the red tape and also to get projects or developments to development, to the end, to building affordable housing. That's something they should look at. How do we leverage our dollars—the existing dollars that we have—and get developers, communities, local CDCs and everyone come together and master plan a city—including in the neighborhood—of how we attack lack of resources or sufficient resources to take those dollars and make them in a way that it's bringing a better neighborhood, better schools, better parks, and better community involvement, and less crime in those neighborhoods?"

2.) More Holistic Public Policy Approach

One of the biggest obstacles to effective national housing policy is the failure of many policy-makers and legislators to treat housing as a multi-dimensional issue, as one that inherently transcends social welfare public policy boundaries. Siloed thinking about housing will always invite failure or inadequate outcomes because housing is never a siloed issue where it matters most: on the streets of distressed communities or in the lives of their residents.

The lack of stable affordable housing for those who suffer through the problem is all too often also a health issue, a jobs issue, an education issue, a transportation issue, a crime issue, and so forth.

Piecemeal housing policy strategy will only produce piecemeal results. Holistic policy approaches—bringing together multiple cabinet-level departments to create new cross-agency initiatives— absolutely has to be part of the foundation upon which we develop and implement national housing policy reform. Such departments, among possibly others, would need to include the U.S. Department of Education, the U.S. Department of Health & Human Services, the Veterans Administration, the U.S. Department of Transportation, and the Defense Department.

There is certainly precedent for HUD working along with other departments on a range of issues. HUD and the VA already work together today on the HUD-VASH program that fuses together HUD housing vouchers with VA supportive services to assist homeless veterans and their families to find and keep permanent housing.

In 2009, as another example, HUD, the EPA, and the U.S. Department of Transportation established the Partnership for Sustainable Communities to help communities' enhanced access to affordable housing and transportation, while protecting the environment.

HUD has also worked with the U.S. Department of Education and the U.S. Department of Health & Human Services to offer access to tools designed to support state and local partnerships that help homeless service providers, school systems, youth services providers, and early childhood providers work better together.

A more holistic approach to housing policy should result in better policies that target two groups, in particular, who now need special attention and assistance: veterans and Native Americans.

Incredibly, 14,000 HUD-VASH vouchers are currently unused—even though at least 37,000 veterans are now homeless.

And the National Low-Income Housing Coalition has perhaps best summarized the problems that Native Americans face:

> *Native Americans in tribal areas have some of the worst housing needs in the United States. They face high poverty rates and low incomes, overcrowding, lack of plumbing and heat, and unique development issues. Despite the growing need for safe, decent homes, federal investments in afford-able housing on tribal lands have been chronically underfunded for decades,*

particularly in more rural and remote areas. Recent changes to federal Native American housing programs have led to an even greater reduction in resources for communities most in need.[6]

3.) Prioritization of Resident-Focused Strategies

If there is one fundamental lesson that I have learned from 35 years in public housing, it is that housing programs can only succeed if they are tailored not only for general local needs, but also, as much as practically possible, for the specific needs of local residents.

Residents' needs and concerns—which not only can vary from city to city, but also from housing residences to housing residences—have to be always front and center in the minds of local housing leaders.

Leaders need a humanistic approach to interacting with housing residents. They just cannot spend all their time in distant, high ivory towers, assessing housing data numbers. They have to try to be frequently on the ground, in the field, experiencing directly what the lives of these people are actually like.

And that requires frequent visitations to their residences and an ongoing effort—never in a one-off fashion—to cultivate lasting relationships with residents.

Martin Luther King Jr. famously lived in poor tenant housing in Chicago, for a time, so he could better relate to the disadvantaged people for whom he advocated.

I am most proud that I have tried to always practice what I have preached on this matter and have accordingly been able to forge good relationships with so many of the residents for whom I have worked. Over time, building such good relationships is really a key to building good housing communities.

— III —

Lessons in Leadership

*We're put here on Earth to learn our own lessons.
No one can tell you what your lessons are; it is part of your personal
journey to discover them. On these journeys we may be given a lot,
or just a little bit, of the things we must grapple with, but never more
than we can handle.*

Elisabeth Kubler-Ross

– Chapter 13–

Biblical Leadership Principles To Live By

As I mentioned earlier, I spent some time in Japan when my dad was transferred to Yokota Air Force Base. At that time, I also underwent a spiritual transition from having no knowledge about God to beginning to embrace a more Christian-centered faith as a practical part of my life. As a part of this conversion to Christianity, I learned many lessons about leadership from historical figures in the Bible. I began incorporating Biblical-based leadership principles into my life and work.

1. Leaders are strengthened by God's promises and not deterred from doing what is right. In Genesis 6, God is despairing over the wickedness that has overtaken humanity. Reluctantly, he decides to wipe out the human race and start from scratch. Noah, however, is the only one who has not been corrupted. God tells him to build an ark to save him, his family, and the animal life. As he is boarding the ark, God says to him, "for you alone I have seen to be righteous before Me in this time." Literally, the whole world was doing what was wrong. But Noah was strengthened by the promises of God and was not deterred from doing what was right.

2. Leaders embrace the unknown. God approaches Abraham in Genesis 12 and tells him, "Go forth from your country, and from your relatives and from your father's house, to the land which I will show you." In other words, Abraham is instructed to leave his comfort zone and march toward uncertainty. As business leaders, managing risk and uncertainty is a hot topic. Great leaders embrace these challenges, because they know the promised land awaits them on the other side.

3. Leaders are concerned and responsive to problems and endure despite circumstances. The story of Joseph beginning in Genesis 37 is a powerful lesson in overcoming tough circumstances. He was sold into slavery by his jealous brothers, and his father was told that a wild animal killed him. Joseph was framed by his boss's wife and thrown into prison because he refused to sleep with her. He interpreted the dream of a prisoner who had promised Joseph that he would help him get out of jail once he was released. That man was soon released and restored to his position, only to forget about Joseph. In the end, though, Joseph became the leader of all Egypt—second only to the Pharaoh himself. He was concerned and responsive to problems, and when there was a famine, his foresight and planning allowed him to save his family from starvation. When he saw them again, Joseph told his brothers that, though they meant harm, God orchestrated the events to put Joseph in a position to save them. Leaders have a vision and faith that sustains them through difficult times.

4. Leaders are assertive and stick up for their people. Yes, it's true. God has to be very convincing to get Moses to take action in Exodus 3. At first, he gives excuse after excuse as to why he isn't the right guy for the job. When he finally does answer his calling, though, Moses assertively approaches Pharaoh and boldly passes on the iconic message: "Let my people go." The Israelites, Moses' native people, had been enslaved by Egypt. Moses was the one enlisted to lead them to freedom. When the time came, Moses was willing to step up, be assertive, and lead. Leaders must use their power and positions to empower and inspire others.

5. Leaders learn to wait on God and rule by example rather than command. After leading his people into a new land, Joshua offers the Israelites two choices: Serve the God who had brought them into the land or serve the gods of the surrounding lands (Joshua 24). "But as for me and my house," Joshua says, "we will serve the Lord."

The people answer in unison that they will pledge their allegiance to God. Because they believe in Joshua's leadership, they follow his example. Still, the Israelites often took two steps forward and one step backward, causing Joshua to have to learn patience and to wait on God. A leader doesn't have to threaten them; he/she merely inspires their followers by setting a good example.

6. Leaders are not afraid of giants. Everybody knows this story. In 1 Samuel 17, the Israelites are being defeated by the Philistines and their nine-foot giant, Goliath. He taunts the Israelites and challenges them to send him one man to fight him with the condition that if that man defeats him, the Philistines will become their servants. David, a small shepherd boy who could not even fit into the over-sized armor he is given, volunteers. When Goliath mocks him, David says, "You come to me with a sword, a spear, and a javelin, but I come to you in the name of the Lord of hosts, whom you have taunted." With that, he takes a stone, slings it at Goliath's forehead, and knocks the giant to the ground dead. The lesson here is that you can face any challenge as long as you have conviction and strength of resolve on your side.

7. Leaders rise to the occasion. In a vision recorded in the Old Testament book of Isaiah, chapter 6, God asks whom he should send as a prophet to His people. Isaiah responds, "Here am I. Send me!" Leaders don't wait to see if anyone else is going to step up when something needs to be done. They take the initiative and are the first to raise their hands. They are the first to stand, to speak up, and to make decisions. Leaders shun inaction and are always ready to take the plunge at a moment's notice.

8. Leaders maintain their resolve without regard for consequences, and they are in constant prayer. Many of us know the story of Daniel in the lion's den recorded in Daniel 6. Daniel is a highly esteemed government official whose colleagues become jealous. They seek to get rid of him, and knowing that he is a religious man, convince the king to enact a decree. The degree says that prayer can be made to no one except the king. Once the decree is issued, Daniel continues his usual routine of praying and giving thanks to God. When he is caught, his colleagues tell their king, who is forced to throw Daniel into a den of lions. The next morning, the king finds Daniel still alive, because the lions had not harmed him. Daniel's faith in his God and devotion to prayer are what made him great in the first place. Knowing this, he would not recant regardless of what happened to him. Great leaders follow Daniel's example and remain steadfast in their convictions regardless of the consequences.

9. Leaders aren't afraid to call out phonies. In Matthew 3, John the Baptist is baptizing people and preaching about the coming of Jesus. When a pretentious, self-righteous group of religious officials come for baptism, he calls them out for what they are: "a brood of vipers." Leaders aren't afraid to tell it like it is. Whether they are talking to suppliers, employees, or even customers, leaders have what it takes to be brutally honest with people.

10. Leaders are servants. One of the most powerful images in the life of Jesus is when he washes his disciples' feet in John 13. When he is finished, he says to them, "You call me teacher and Lord, and you are right, for so I am. If I then, the Lord and teacher, washed your feet, you also ought to wash one another's feet." Jesus is talking about servant-leadership. Great leaders focus on serving those who follow them. Great leaders wash their people's feet.

11. Leaders recover from failure and identify with the failures of others. The most well-known disciple of Jesus, Peter, denies even knowing Him three times while Jesus is being tried and crucified. Jesus had predicted Peter's denials, even though Peter insisted he would never deny Jesus, even to the death. When the rooster crowed three times (what Jesus said would happen), Peter realized what he had done and wept bitterly. Fast forward to Acts 2, where we see Peter giving the first sermon after Jesus' ascension into heaven. He spoke powerfully to thousands of people, just days after denying he knew Jesus, possibly to some of the same people. Leaders don't become discouraged when they fail or when others fail them. They don't wallow in self-pity and give up due to the mishap but vow to do better next time. They pick themselves back up and continue.

12. Leaders are passionate about what they believe in. Throughout his life as recorded in the book of Acts, Paul is a zealous individual. As a Pharisee, he violently opposed the spread of Christianity. He went out of his way to see that Christians were killed and imprisoned. When Jesus appeared to him in Acts 9 and changed his mind, Paul became equally adamant about the truth of Christianity. After his conversion, he traveled all over the known world, spreading the message about Jesus, and establishing churches everywhere he went. Like Paul, leaders are driven by a sense of purpose. Leaders have a fire lit under them and feel compelled to accomplish their objectives. There is no place for apathy in the life of a leader. Leaders always care and care deeply.

I selected the Biblical leaders above because each provided a lesson that was invaluable to my work in housing authorities. As you have read in the previous chapters, each housing authority in the US and Canada came with many challenges, obstacles and opportunities. Learning about Christ and how he selected, taught and corrected the twelve disciples gave me the perfect modules to educate and encourage my staff in each of the cities where I served. It also provided a roadmap for how I needed to relate to public officials and, above all else, residents. It is love, respect, and caring that made a difference in my achievements because I put others' needs, interests and concerns before mine.

My relationship and dependence on Christ's teaching sensitized me to the importance of the spiritual aspect of employing a holistic approach to housing humans. Therefore, faith-based organizations and ministries need to rethink their mission to the poorest of the poor in the US, particularly in the pandemic age. Offering hope and having faith is essential to the horrid survival before, during, and aftermaths of this pandemic. The only way to help residents have hope and hang on to faith is by housing authority leaders and their staff learning to "Love the least of our brothers as we love ourselves."

– Chapter 14 –

Takeaways from the Air Force

The Air Force provided my family—and later me—an opportunity to live in multiple countries, American states, and cities. Past generations would call us "citizens of the world," but today, this growing population is identified as Global Cosmopolitans.

In her book *Global Cosmopolitans, The Creative Edge of Difference*, Linda Brimm offers this observation about Global Cosmopolitans:

> *Many of them come from humble immigrant backgrounds, grew up in multiple countries, speaking various languages, and have had to work very hard to get where they are today. Some are simply from bicultural families and have been born into a world of globalization and change. While their international identities have diverse starting points and experiences, their views of the world and themselves are profoundly affected by both the realities of living in different cultures and their manner of coping with the challenges that emerge.*[1]

Critical lessons

Global Cosmopolitans are remarkably good at learning from life experiences; although, they often don't realize it themselves. Their skills can provide all of us with critical lessons that can help us maximize our potential. A global cosmopolitan mindset consists of three parts: a growth mindset, a global mindset, and a creative mindset.

Global Cosmopolitans often say attitudes help substantially in new situations where they have to deal with the complications of difference. Those attitudes were formed by thinking of their lives as an opportunity to learn and grow. A growth mindset helps Global Cosmopolitans remain flexible and open to change. It forms the basis for finding creative solutions to the complications of global life and work. On the other hand, having a rigid mindset, such as having clear rules about right and wrong, or good and evil, can help them feel secure but limit their ability to grow. Having a learning orientation often kick-starts a virtuous cycle: The creativity they cultivate feeds back into their motivation to continue learning.

My Air Force training and overseas and U.S. assignments helped me develop skills and acquire qualities that served me well in leading nine U.S. housing authorities and one in Toronto, Canada.

Skills

During my time in the Air Force, I learned the importance of humor, mentorship, communication skills, and problem-solving cognitive processes. I learned how to harmonize actions at the three levels of war, sociability, and a preference for relationship building, cross-cultural and language capabilities, and an understanding of organizations.

A leader must think critically, strategically, and creatively to meet both present and future challenges. In addition, visionary leadership incorporates creative interventions to processes, technological developments, and keeping up with emerging challenges.

Strategic thinking is an ongoing activity where leaders regularly scan the current environments seeking a glimpse of possible futures. A dose of creative thinking supported by critical thinking skills helps the leader in this endeavor.

Future leaders must have and refine networking skills to meet and keep track of potential teammates and allies across a broad range of constituencies. Officers must cultivate these skills early in their careers. Such leaders must be comfortable serving as facilitators and negotiators. These personal skills enable future leaders to work effectively across the bounds of services, countries, and cultures. They must have experience in building partnerships, both in and out of the Air Force, and be skilled in collaborating with peers, other services, interagency organizations, and coalition partners.

More recently, the rise of regional policy in the post-Cold War era transformed regional combatant commanders into critical players in defense policymaking. Part of this transformation has been an increased emphasis on partnership building and alliances.

Since senior appointments, such as regional commands, must be confirmed by Congress, the ability to skillfully navigate Capitol Hill must be considered part of this leader's skill set. They also must remain apolitical while striving to be politically savvy.

Future leaders must also be culturally astute and skilled negotiators. In their discussion of Army strategic leadership competencies, Dr. Leonard Wong and his colleagues at the U.S. Army War College describe the meta competency "cross-cultural savvy" as the ability to work with non-U.S. militaries as well as "the ability to understand cultures beyond one's organizational, economic, religious, societal, geographical, and political boundaries."[2]

Air Force leaders must have skills to work with their counterparts in other services, government agencies, non-governmental organizations, and other countries. Since senior leaders often are charged with mission success, that requires working with people over whom they have no direct authority. The ability to resolve issues through persuasion and influence is key to their negotiation skills set.

Given the future's uncertainty, fast pace, huge amounts of often-conflicting data, and rapidly shifting dynamics, future leaders must have coping skills to meet the wide range of challenges. They must be willing to access a variety of resources to help them, and their subordinates cope with the emotional and psychological rigors of the VUCA environment.

Future leaders must be able to assess conflicting resource requests and allocate limited resources to most effectively support the enterprise's overall strategy. This characteristic—always important—is even more so in an increasingly resource-constrained environment.

Qualities

Cognitive characteristics relate to conscious intellectual activity. Future leaders are self-aware and possess a high level of metacognition. Conscious and critical of their own thought processes, they can step back and view problems and proposed solutions from a detached perspective.

Visionary leadership is transformative and based on the power of inspiration. It is often characterized by a commitment to core values, clear visions, and respect for empowering relationships and facilitated by courageous and innovative action.

Following the example of U.S. Army resiliency training, leaders must be dedicated to both mental and emotional stability and physical fitness, so they may thrive in an era of high operational tempos and persistent conflict. Future leaders must rely on a strong ethical basis on which their selflessness and humility can flourish.

As General Montgomery Meigs explained in his article on generalship, "Good generals are not worried about themselves when they make the tough decisions. They must be willing to share information, to encourage frank and open dialogue, and to approach issues with a broad, problem-solving perspective to convey mission goals to a diverse group of stakeholders, allies, and others." Instruction on how to negotiate will soon be added to the U.S. Army's leader development program.[3]

Future leaders mentor their replacements and share their ideas and philosophies for the future with others.

Training

A lifelong endeavor of learning and continuous self-improvement must be part of every leader's psyche. "The officer profession must commit itself to a lifetime of dedicated study of strategy, politics, economics, and history. Future leaders are those who are always open to learning."[4]

Edgar Puryear described the habit of avid reading as one of the hallmarks of a successful senior officer. Thus, future leaders hone their writing and speaking skills over a lifetime of reading, listening, practice, and delivery.[5]

– Chapter 15–

The North Star

The reader will note not all my policy viewpoints fit into the liberal Democratic box.

While my views are much more closely aligned with the Democratic Party, I am most certainly not an ideologue nor an extreme partisan and am much more interested in viable solutions than mindless conformity to some ideological orthodoxy.

Most Americans are pragmatic, as I am, and really don't care which side of the spectrum the solutions to our problems originate as long as they can solve problems or, at least, mitigate them. Perhaps Franklin Roosevelt described best the kind of open-minded, practical approach that all policymakers should follow when doing their jobs. During the worst days of the Great Depression, President Roosevelt was asked to explain the ideological nature of the New Deal's Tennessee Valley Authority, which brought electric power to millions. "I'll tell them it's neither fish nor fowl," he remarked. "But whatever it is, it will taste awfully good to the people of the Tennessee Valley."[1]

Unfortunately, too often today in public policy, it is terribly difficult to project a long-term vision for reform because, frequently, short-term distractions and seemingly endless partisan, factional and ideological conflicts distort the public vision and impede our capacity to project ahead and lay the groundwork for needed change. As it is, developing a vision for reform is the *easy* part. And there are certainly no shortages of good proposals on the table for reform of U.S. housing policy—but there are shortages of action needed to make those proposals a reality.

National housing policy reform today will thus require not just detailed policy plans and proposals, but a strong, durable political will to convert them into law and/or through the necessary executive and administrative orders. To ensure the successful impact of such new laws and reformed policies, we will also need to thread the policy needle.

We need to strengthen federal oversight of public housing programs, to ensure compliance with law and to preclude waste and fraud. However, we must also decentralize authority to maximize local flexibility in the administration of programs, creating ample new breathing space for innovation tailored for local needs.

Ultimately, the essential imperative for national housing policy must always be a laser-beam focus on delivering tangible results that can be most deeply felt by those most desperately in need in our distressed communities. That, above all else, should be our North Star for national housing policy reform, our guiding principle, our roadmap.

Let us find common ground to create a reformed national housing policy that produces not just **good buildings but good homes, not just good tenants but good citizens, and not just foundations that support brick and steel, but foundations that support thriving communities.**

Endnotes

page v:
1. Maslow, Abraham, *Motivation and Personality,* New York: Harper & Brothers *1954*

Preface:
1. https://www.whitehouse.gov/sites/whitehouse.gov/files/images/ Housing_Development_Toolkit%20f.2.pdf.
2. Ibid.

Chapter 2:
1. https://www.airforce.com/education/military-training.
2. http://leadership.au.af.mil/af/afldm.htm.
3. Ibid.
4. Ibid.
5. https://www.desertusa.com/cities/ca/victorville-ca.html.
6. https://www.afcec.af.mil/Home/BRAC/George.aspx.
7. https://en.wikipedia.org/wiki/Rhein-Main_Air_Base.
8. https://www.nytimes.com/1976/06/17/archives/us-ambassador- and-aide-kidnapped-and-murdered-in-beirut-combat.html.

Chapter 3:
1. https://www.history.com/topics/natural-disasters-and-environ ment/1989-san-francisco-earthquake.
2. https://en.wikipedia.org/wiki/Oakland_firestorm_of_1991.
3. Jackman, Tom, "KC housing receiver is named." Kansas City Star, 26 August 1994

Chapter 5:

1. https://www.iweathernet.com/tropical/hurricane-katrina-the- dire-warning-that-saved-lives.

Chapter 5. continued:

2. "Katrina Heads for New Orleans." Fox News/Associated Press. August 29, 2005.
3. Drye, Willie. "Hurricane Katrina Pulls Its Punches in New Orleans." National Geographic. August 29, 2005.
4. "Washing Away: Special Report from The Times-Picayune." Times-Picayune. June 23–27, 2002. Archived November 12, 2005, at Archive-It.
5. https://www.britannica.com/event/Hurricane-Katrina.
6. Ibid.
7. https://archives.hud.gov/news/2006/pr06-018.cfm .
8. Ibid.
9. https://www.hano.org/our_story.aspx.
10. Ibid.
11. Ibid.
12. https://www.governing.com/gov-revisiting-hope-public-housing-programs-legacy.html.
13. https://www.oig.dhs.gov/assets/Mgmt/OIG_06-32_Mar06.pdf
14. https://www.hano.org/our_story.aspx.

Chapter 6:

1. https://www.hano.org/our_story.aspx.
2. https://www.chicagotribune.com/news/ct-xpm-2005-07-17-0507170436-story.html.
3. wikipedia.org/wiki/Kwame Kilpatrick.

Chapter 7:

1. https://www.thestar.com/news/gta/2012/05/08/tchc_reaches_across_border_to_pick_a_new_ceo.html.
2. Ibid.
3. https://nationalpost.com/posted-toronto/i-dont-operate-this-agency-from-behind-the-desk-ceo-of-canadas-largest-landlord-aims-to-restore-credibility.
4. Ibid.
5. https://www.thestar.com/news/gta/2012/09/28/fiorito_a_new_broom_at_tchc.html.
6. Ibid.

7. https://www.thestar.com/news/city_hall/2014/02/13/tchc_
    president_keeps_his_job_but_bonus_gets_cut.html.
8. Ibid.
9. https://www.theglobeandmail.com/news/toronto/tchc/
    article18207461/.
10. Ibid.
11. Ibid.
12. Ibid.
13. Ibid.
14. Ibid.

Chapter 8:
1. http://don411.com/mayor-emanuel-and-chicago-housing-
    authority-board-chair-z-scott-announce-eugene-jones-as-
    acting-ceo-of-the-cha-jose-alvarez-to-be-promoted-to-
    chief-of-staff-new-leadership-team-reaffirms-commit
    ment/#.XcVrWjNKjIU.
2. https://www.chicago.gov/city/en/depts/mayor/press_room/
    press_releases/2016/february/Drive-Neighborhood-
    Development.html.
3. https://www.youtube.com/watch?v=Rm7PY4gEyB8&t=3s.
4. https://www.youtube.com/watch?v=YN8lQ71yJnU.
5. https://www.youtube.com/watch?v=Rm7PY4gEyB8&t=2507s.
6. Ibid.
7. https://www.youtube.com/watch?v=szhkUnZfkK8.
8. Ibid.
9. Ibid.
10. https://chicagocrusader.com/cha-in-flux-after-resignations/.
11. https://chicago.curbed.com/2019/8/21/20827053/chicago-
    housing-authority-resign-ceo-eugene-jones.
12. https://www.wbez.org/shows/wbez-news/chicago-housing-
    authority-ceo-eugene-jones-resigns/9e44aff8-7b15-4f69-
    a6d7-82162a9d9d3a.
13. https://www.google.com/search?q=Pat+Dowell&o
    q=Pat+Dowell&aqs=chrome..69i57j69i60.948j0j7&
    sourceid=chrome&ie=UTF-8.

Chapter 9:

1. https://www.ajc.com/news/former-head-chicago-housing-tapped-lead-atlanta-housing-authority/EWRqTKZh6Dnlqtwo5yoNJM/.
2. https://www.theatlantavoice.com/articles/atlanta-housing-authority-appoints-eugene-jones-as-new-ceo/.
3. Ibid.
4. https://www.ajc.com/news/former-head-chicago-housing-tapped-lead-atlanta-housing-authority/EWRqTKZh6Dnlqtwo5yoNJM/.
5. https://www.theatlantavoice.com/articles/a-matter-of-urgency-atlanta-housing-ceo-eugene-jones-aligns-with-mayors-vision-to-make-affordable-housing-top-priority/.
6. Ibid.
7. https://saportareport.com/giving-thanks-for-the-uplifting-moments-in-our-lives/.
8. https://www.wabe.org/new-atlanta-housing-ceo-eugene-jones-talks-affordability-partnerships-section-8-laws/.
9. Ibid.
10. https://www.theatlantavoice.com/articles/atlanta-housing-authority-appoints-eugene-jones-as-new-ceo/.
11. https://www.hud.gov/section3.
12. https://www.westsidefuturefund.org/news/a-conversation-with-atlanta-housing-ceo-eugene-jones-jr/.
13. Ibid.
14. https://saportareport.com/breaking-avoiding-a-trial-atlanta-housing-board-approves-amended-settlement-agreement-with-integral-group-partners.
15. https://www.washingtonpost.com/realestate/the-noah-conundrum-maintaining-the-lifeboat-for-affordable-rental-housing/2020/03/18/e3e18aa6-12ba-11ea-bf62-eadd5d11f559_story.html.
16. https://saportareport.com/watch-atlanta-housing-ceo-addresses-trump-administrations-efforts-to-eliminate-public-housing/.

17. https://www.wsbtv.com/news/local/mayor-city-offering-rent-help-residents-living-atlanta-housing/MR567Y2EAZD3PLBQTQ7CLOW4CM/.
18. Ibid.

Chapter 11:
1. https://reports.nlihc.org/gap.
2. Ibid.
3. Ibid.
4. https://www.brookings.edu/blog/up-front/2020/06/01/housing-hardships-reach-unprecedented-heights-during-the-covid-19-pandemic/.
5. https://www.cbpp.org/three-out-of-four-low-income-at-risk-renters-do-not-receive-federal-rental-assistance.
6. Scally Corianne, Payton; Batko, Samantha; Popkin, Susan J.; DuBois, Nicole, "The Case for More, Not Less Shortfalls in Federal Housing Assistance and Gaps in Evidence for Proposed Policy Changes," The Urban Institute Research Report, 2018, 8.
7. https://www.urban.org/sites/default/files/publication/101482/the_future_of_public_housing_public_housing_fact_sheet_1.pdf
8. https://nlihc.org/resource/2019-ameri can-housing-survey-data-now-available.
9. Ibid.
10. https://www.nahb.org/News-and-Economics/Housing-Economics/Indices/Housing-Opportunity-Index.
11. https://www.nhlp.org/campaign/protecting-renter-and-home owner-rights-during-our-national-health-crisis-2/.
12. https://www.aspeninstitute.org/blog-posts/americas-looming-eviction-crisis/.
13. https://nlihc.org/resource/analysis-president-trumps-fy2020-budget-request.
14. https://www.npr.org/2020/07/21/893471887/seeking-suburban-votes-trump-targets-rule-to-combat-racial-bias-in-housing.

Chapter 11 continued.

15. https://www.nar.realtor/newsroom/nar-disappointed-in-administrations-final-affirmatively-furthering-fair-housing-rule.
16. https://homesnow.org/short-history-of-public-housing-in-the-us-1930s-present/.
17. Ibid.
18. https://www.hud.gov/sites/documents/LEGS_CHRON_JUNE2014.PDF.
19. https://en.wikipedia.org/wiki/Housing_and_Urban_Development_Act_of_1965#.
20. https://www.hud.gov/sites/documents/LEGS_CHRON_JUNE2014.PDF.
21. https://www.cbpp.org/research/housing/federal-policy-changes-can-help-more-families-with-housing-vouchers-live-in-higher.
22. https://nlihc.org/resource/housing-subsidies-lift-29-million-out-poverty#.
23. https://www.healthaffairs.org/do/10.1377/hpb 20180313.396577/full/.
24. Fenelon, Andrew, Natalie Slopen, Michel Boudreaux, Sandra J. Newman. "The Impact of Housing Assistance on the Mental Health of Children in the United States," Journal of Health and Social Behavior, Volume 59: issue 3, 2018: 447-463.
25. Ibid.
26. "Trends in Housing Assistance and Who It Serves. 2019 Housing Impact Report," Public and Affordable Housing Research Corporation (PAHRC), 3. https://www.housingcenter.com/wp-content/uploads/2019/06/Housing-Impact-Report-2019.pdf.
27. Scally Corianne, Payton; Batko, Samantha; Popkin, Susan J.; DuBois, Nicole, "The Case for More, Not Less Shortfalls in Federal Housing Assistance and Gaps in Evidence for Proposed Policy Changes," The Urban Institute Research Report, 2018, 3.

28. "Trends in Housing Assistance and Who It Serves. 2019 Housing Impact Report," Public and Affordable Housing Research Corporation (PAHRC), 3.
29. Scally, et, al.
30. "Trends in Housing Assistance and Who It Serves. 2019 Housing Impact Report," Public and Affordable Housing Research Corporation (PAHRC), 3.

Chapter 12:
1. https://nmtccoalition.org/fact-sheet/.
2. Technical Preservation Services, "Tax Incentives for Preserving Historic Properties," U.S. National Park Service: https://www.nps.gov/tps/tax-incentives.htm.
3. Sard, Barbara; Thrope, Deborah, "Consolidating Rental Assistance Administration Would Increase Efficiency and Expand Opportunity," Policy Futures, Center on Budget and Policy Priorities, 2016, 1.
4. Ibid.
5. Ibid.
6. "Native American Housing," National Low Income Housing Coalition: https://nlihc.org/explore-issues/policy-priorities/native-american-housing.

Chapter 14:
1. Brimm, Linda (2010). *Global Cosmopolitans, The Creative Edge of Difference.* Insead Business Press Series, Palgrave Macmillan. p. 4. ISBN 978-0230230781.
2. Wong, Leonard, et. al. "Strategic Leadership Competencies." PDF found at https://publications.armywarcollege.edu/pubs/1677.pdf.
3. Currie, Karen, et. al. "Air Force Leadership Study: The Need for Deliberate Development." Found at: https://www.jstor.org/stable/resrep13757.9.
4. Ibid.
5. Ibid.

Chapter 15:

1. https:// www.usnews.com/news/articles/2015/04/09/1933
-the-rise-of-the-common-man.

Sources Cited

Authored Works:

Alcoba, Natalie. "'I don't operate this agency from behind the desk': New head of TCHC aims to restore credibility." *National Post*, 28 July 28 2012. https://nationalpost.com/posted-toronto/i-dont-operate-this-agency-from-behind-the-desk-ceo-of-canadas-largest-landlord-aims-to-restore-credibility.

Burress, Jim. " New Atlanta Housing CEO Eugene Jones Talks Affordability, Partnerships, Section 8 Laws." 1*WABE*. 9 November 2019. https://www.wabe.org/new-atlanta-housing-ceo-eugene-jones-talks-affordability-partnerships-section-8-laws/.

Currie, Karen, John Conway, Scott Johnson, Brian Landry, and Adam Lowther. "Air Force Leadership Study: The Need for Deliberate Development." Report. Air University Press, 2012. http://www.jstor.org/stable/resrep13757.9.

Dale Daniel, Paul Moloney. "TCHC CEO Gene Jones denied bonus, forced to go back to school." *Toronto Star*, 13 February 2014. https://www.thestar.com/news/city_hall/2014/02/13/tchc_president_keeps_his_job_but_bonus_gets_cut.html.

Drye, Willie. "Hurricane Katrina Pulls Its Punches in New." *National Geographic*, 29 August 2005.

Fenelon, Andrew, Natalie Slopen, Michel Boudreaux, and Sandra J. Newman. "The Impact of Housing Assistance." *Journal of Health and Social Behavior* 59 (3) 2018: 447-463.

Fiorito, Joe. "Fiorito: A new broom at TCHC." *Toronto Star*, 28 September 2012.

Grinstein-Wiess Michal, Brinda Gupta, Yung Chun, Hedwig Lee, and Mathieu Despard. "Housing hardships reach unprecedented heights during the Covid-19 pandemic." *Brookings*. n.d. https://www.brookings.edu/blog/up-front/2020/06/01/housing-hardships-reach-unprecedented-heights-during-the-covid-19-pandemic/.

Hui, Ann. "Rob Ford ally out as TCHC boss after scathing ombudsman's report." *The Globe and Mail*, 25 April 2014. https://www.theglobeandmail.com/news/toronto/tchc/article18207461/.

Jackman, Tom. "KC housing receiver is named." *The Kansas City Star*, 26 August 1994: C1, C2.

Keenan, Sean. "BREAKING: Avoiding a trial, Atlanta Housing board approves amended settlement agreement with Integral Group, partners." *Saporta Report*. 26 February 2020. https://saportareport.com/breaking-avoiding-a-trial-atlanta-housing-board-approves-amended-settlement-agreement-with-integral-group-partners/.

Latimore, Marshall. "Atlanta Housing CEO Eugene Jones aligns with Mayor's vision to make affordable housing top priority." *Atlanta Voice*. 13 March 2020. https://www.theatlantavoice.com/articles/a-matter-of-urgency-atlanta-housing-ceo-eugene-jones-aligns-with-mayors-vision-to-make-affordable-housing-top-priority/.

Mckay, Katherine Lucas. "The Aspen Institute Insight: America's Looming Eviction Crisis." *Aspen Institute*. 28 August 2020. https://www.aspeninstitute.org/blog-posts/americas-looming-eviction-crisis/.

MacFarlane, Cathy. "JACKSON OUTLINES HUD'S RESPONSE TO HURRICANE KATRINA IN TESTIMONY BEFORE SENATE BANKING COMMITTEE: HUD Secretary vows 'HUD's in this for the long haul'". *U.S. Department of Housing and Urban Development*. 15 February 2001. https://archives.hud.gov/news/2006/pr06-018.cfm.

Markham, James. "U.S. AMBASSADOR AND AIDE KIDNAPPED AND MURDERED IN BEIRUT COMBAT SECTOR." *The New York Times*, 17 June 1976: 1. https://www.nytimes.com/1976/06/17/archives/us-ambassador-and-aide-kidnapped-and-murdered-in-beirut-combat.html.

Maslow, Abraham, *Motivation and Personality*, New York: Harper & Brothers, 1954.

Moore, Natalie. "Chicago Housing Authority CEO Eugene Jones Resigns." *WBEZ*. 21 August 2019. https://www.wbez.org/stories/chicago-housing-authority-ceo-eugene-jones-resigns/9e44aff8-7b15-4f69-a6d7-82162a9d9d3a.

Robbins, Chris. "Hurricane Katrina: The Dire NWS Warning That Saved Lives." *IWeather*. 28 August 2015. https://www.iweathernet.com/tropical/hurricane-katrina-the-dire-warning-that-saved-lives.

Saporta, Maria. "Giving thanks for the uplifting moments in our lives." *Saporta Report*. 25 November 2019. https://saportareport.com/giving-thanks-for-the-uplifting-moments-in-our-lives/.

Sard, Barbara, and Deborah Thrope. "Consolidating Rental Assistance Administration Would Increase Efficiency and Expand Opportunity." *Center on Budget and Policy Priorities*. 11 April 2016. https://www.cbpp.org/research/housing/consolidating-rental-assistance-administration-would-increase-efficiency-and-expand.

Scally Corianne, Payton, Samantha Batko, Susan J. Popkin, and Nicole DuBois. "The Case for More, Not Less Shortfalls in Federal Housing Assistance and Gaps in Evidence for Proposed Policy Changes." *Urban Institue*. 4 January 2018. https://www.urban.org/research/publication/case-more-not-less-shortfalls-federal-housing-assistance-and-gaps-evidence-proposed-policy-changes.

Sharpe, Martel. "Atlanta Housing Authority appoints Eugene Jones as new CEO." *Atlanta Voice.* 12 September 2019. https://www.theatlantavoice.com/articles/atlanta-housing-authority-appoints-eugene-jones-as-new-ceo/.

Suggs, Ernie. "Former head of Chicago housing tapped to lead Atlanta Housing Authority." *Atlanta Journal-Constitution,* 10 September 2019. https://www.ajc.com/news/former-head-chicago-housing-tapped-lead-atlanta-housing-authority/EWRqTKZh6Dnlqtwo5yoNJM/.

Suzette Hackney and Marisol Bello, Knight Ridder/Tribune: Detroit Free Press. Contributors: Ben Schmitt, Kathleen Gray and Jennifer Dixon. "Feds to oversee Detroit's public housing agency." *Chicago Tribune.* 17 July 2005. https://www.chicagotribune.com/news/ct-xpm-2005-07-17-0507170436-story.html.

Taylor, Lauren. "Housing And Health: An Overview Of The Literature." *Health Affairs.* 7 June 2018. https://www.healthaffairs.org/do/10.1377/hpb20180313.396577/.

Trenkner, Tina. "Revisiting the Hope VI Public Housing Program's Legacy." 2012. *Governing.* https://www.governing.com/gov-revisiting-hope-public-housing-programs-legacy.html.

Vincent, Donovan. "TCHC reaches across border to pick a new CEO." *The Star.* 8 May 2012. https://www.thestar.com/news/gta/2012/05/08/tchc_reaches_across_border_to_pick_a_new_ceo.html.

Willis, Haisten. "Preserving Affordable Housing." *The Washington Post.* 19 March 2020.. https://www.washingtonpost.com/realestate/the-noah-conundrum-maintaining-the-lifeboat-for-affordable-rental-housing/2020/03/18/e3e18aa6-12ba-11ea-bf62-eadd5d11f559_story.html.

Websites, No Author Noted:

Air Force Civil Engineer Center. "Former George Air Force Base (BRAC 1992)." n.d. https://www.afcec.af.mil/Home/BRAC/George.aspx.

Associated Press. "Katrina Heads for New Orleans." 29 August 2005. https://www.foxnews.com/story/katrina-heads-for-new-orleans.

Center on Budget and Policy Priorities. "Three Out of Four Low-Income At-Risk Renters Do Not Receive Federal Rental Assistance." n.d. https://www.cbpp.org/three-out-of-four-low-income-at-risk-renters-do-not-receive-federal-rental-assistance.

"Federal Policy Changes Can Help More Families with Housing Vouchers Live in Higher-Opportunity Areas." 4 September 2018. https://www.cbpp.org/research/housing/federal-policy-changes-can-help-more-families-with-housing-vouchers-live-in-higher.

Chicago: Office of the Mayor. 2016. "Mayor Emanuel Announces Major Initiative to Further Drive Neighborhood Development." 28 February 2016. https://www.chicago.gov/city/en/depts/mayor/press_room/press_releases/2016/february/Drive-Neighborhood-Development.html.

Chicago Crusader. "CHA in flux after resignations." 22 August 2019. https://chicagocrusader.com/cha-in-flux-after-resignations/.

DesertUSA. "Victorville, California: A Crossroad in History." n.d. https://www.desertusa.com/cities/ca/victorville-ca.html.

Don411. "MAYOR EMANUEL AND CHICAGO HOUSING
    AUTHORITY BOARD CHAIR Z SCOTT ANNOUNCE
    EUGENE JONES AS ACTING CEO OF THE CHA; Jose
    Alvarez To Be Promoted to Chief of Staff; New Leadership
    Team Reaffirms Commitment to Build New Housing
    Opportunities Outlined in the 2012." n.d. https://don411.
    com/mayor-emanuel-and-chicago-housing-authority-
    board-chair-z-scott-announce-eugene-jones-as-acting-ceo-
    of-the-cha-jose-alvarez-to-be-promoted-to-chief-of-staff-
    new-leadership-team-reaffirms-commitment/.

Encyclopedia Britannica. "Hurricane Katrina". 17 July 2008. https://
    www.britannica.com/event/Hurricane-Katrina.

History. "1989 San Francisco Earthquake." https://www.history.
    com/topics/natural-disasters-and-environment/1989-san-
    francisco-earthquake-video.

Homes NOW, Not Later. "Short History of Public Housing in the
    US (1930's – Present)" n.d. https://homesnow.org/short-
    history-of-public-housing-in-the-us-1930s-present/.

National Association of Home Builders. "NAHB/Wells Fargo
    Housing Opportunity Index (HOI). https://www.nahb.
    org/News-and-Economics/Housing-Economics/Indices/
    Housing-Opportunity-Index.

National Association of Realtors. "NAR Disappointed in
    Administration's Final Affirmatively Furthering Fair
    Housing Rule." 23 July 2020. https://www.nar.realtor/
    newsroom/nar-disappointed-in-administrations-final-
    affirmatively-furthering-fair-housing-rule.

National Housing Law Project. "Protecting Renter and Homeowner
    Rights During Our National Health Crisis." 23 September
    2020. https://www.nhlp.org/campaign/protecting-renter-
    and-homeowner-rights-during-our-national-health-
    crisis-2/.

National Low Income Housing Coalition. "2019 American Housing Survey Data Now Available." 21 September 2020. https://nlihc.org/resource/2019-american-housing-survey-data-now-available.

"Analysis of President Trump's FY2020 Budget Request." 11 March 2019. https://nlihc.org/resource/analysis-president-trumps-fy2020-budget-request.

"Housing Subsidies Lift 2.9 Million Out of Poverty." 17 September 2018. https://nlihc.org/resource/housing-subsidies-lift-29-million-out-poverty#.

"Native American Housing." n.d. https://nlihc.org/explore-issues/policy-priorities/native-american-housing.

"The Gap: A Shortage of Affordable Rentable Homes." n.d. https://reports.nlihc.org/gap.

New Markets Tax Credit Coalition. "New Markets Tax Credit Fact Sheet." n.d. https://nmtccoalition.org/fact-sheet/.

NPR. "Seeking Suburban Votes, Trump To Repeal Rule Combating Racial Bias In Housing." 21 July 2020. https://www.npr.org/2020/07/21/893471887/seeking-suburban-votes-trump-targets-rule-to-combat-racial-bias-in-housing.

Public and Affordable Housing Research Corporation. "Trends in Housing Assistance and Who It Serves." 2019. PDF found at: https://www.housingcenter.com/wp-content/uploads/2019/06/Housing-Impact-Report-2019.pdf.

Saporta Report. "WATCH: Atlanta Housing CEO addresses 'Trump administration's efforts to eliminate public housing.' 5 February 2020. https://saportareport.com/watch-atlanta-housing-ceo-addresses-trump-administrations-efforts-to-eliminate-public-housing/.

U.S. Air Force. *U.S. Air Force - Military Training.* n.d. https://www.
airforce.com/education/military-training.

U.S. Department of Homeland Security. "A Performance Review
of FEMA's Disaster Management Activities in Response to
Hurricane Katrina." March 31, 2006. https://www.oig.dhs.
gov/assets/Mgmt/OIG_06-32_Mar06.pdf.

U.S. Deptment of Housing and Urban Development. *About Section
3.* https://www.hud.gov/section3.

"MAJOR LEGISLATION ON HOUSING AND URBAN
DEVELOPMENT ENACTED SINCE 1932." June 2014.
PDF found at: https://www.hud.gov/sites/documents/
LEGS_CHRON_JUNE2014.PDF.

U.S. National Park Service. "Tax Incentives for Preserving Historic
Properties." n.d. https://www.nps.gov/tps/tax-incentives.
htm.

U.S. News. "1933: The Rise of the Common Man". 9 April 2015.
https://www.usnews.com/news/articles/2015/04/09/1933-
the-rise-of-the-common-man.

YouTube: "Eugene E. Jones, Jr., CEO, Chicago Housing Authority."
City Club of Chicago. Chicago, IL, 20 March 2019. https://
www.youtube.com/watch?v=szhkUnZfkK8.

"Eugene Jones, CEO, Chicago Housing Authority." *City
Club of Chicago.* Chicago, IL, 16 April 16 2018. https://www.
youtube.com/watch?v=Rm7PY4gEyB8&t=2507s.

"Eugene Jones, CEO, Chicago Housing Authority." *City Club
of Chicago.* Chicago, IL, 16 April 2018. https://www.youtube.
com/watch?v=Rm7PY4gEyB8&t=3s.

"Eugene Jones, CEO, Chicago Housing Authority." *City Club
of Chicago.* Chicago, IL, 13 June 2016. https://www.youtube.
com/watch?v=YN8lQ71yJnU.

Westside Future Fund. "A Conversation with Atlanta Housing CEO, Eugene Jones, Jr." 4 February 2020. https://www.westsidefuturefund.org/news/a-conversation-with-atlanta-housing-ceo-eugene-jones-jr/.

White House. "Housing Development Toolkit". September 2016. https://www.whitehouse.gov/sites/whitehouse.gov/files/images/Housing_Development_Toolkit%20f.2.pdf.

WSBTV News. "Mayor, city offering rent help for residents living in Atlanta Housing." 7 April 2020. https://www.wsbtv.com/news/local/mayor-city-offering-rent-help-residents-living-atlanta-housing/MR567Y2EAZD3PLBQTQ7CLOW4CM/.

Wikipedia. "Housing and Urban Development Act of 1965." n.d. https://en.wikipedia.org/wiki/Housing_and_Urban_Development_Act_of_1965#.

"Kwame Kilpatrick." n.d. https://en.wikipedia.org/wiki/Kwame_Kilpatrick.

"Oakland firestorm of 1991." n.d. https://en.wikipedia.org/wiki/Oakland_firestorm_of_1991.

"Rhein-Main Air Base." n.d. https://en.wikipedia.org/wiki/Rhein-Main_Air_Base.

Eugene and his Little Brother, Paris Jackson, in San Francisco, 1992.

About the Author

Eugene E. Jones, Jr. is a globally recognized turnaround/recovery expert delivering strong results, while creating public/private business partnerships in this highly regulated housing industry. CEO and President positions have included housing authorities in eight major cities in the United States and Canada.

Gene has a proven track record spanning over 35 years of public housing leadership and experience in management, public/private partnerships, operations, finance and governance in the public housing industry. He's had billion-dollar profit/loss responsibilities for organizations requiring strategic planning, revenue management and risk management. Gene is also responsible for leading and building over $3 billion of housing development structures.

Throughout his public housing service, Gene has demonstrated expertise in transformational leadership—federal, state and local--and public policy. Gene is a servant leader, passionate about empowering others to reach their full potential or to use their voices, and positions to elevate others in need.

Gene has worked in community outreach with numerous organizations in varied roles throughout his life. There is one in particular that he has a deep connection with—Big Brothers Big Sisters of America (BBBS). Gene has been a Big Brother to a Little Brother for over 40 years. **Because of his deep, personal relationship with the BBBS organization, Gene has decided to donate 10% of all book proceeds to the BBBS program. Gene sees the BBBS as a preventative and proactive organization that changes the lives and trajectories of children and their families, giving them the opportunities to reach their full potential.**

CPSIA information can be obtained
at www.ICGtesting.com
Printed in the USA
LVHW092139070221
678675LV00003B/19